MW01225563

10

MINUTE GUIDE TO

INTERNET EXPLORER 4.0

by Joe Lowery

with Joe Habraken, Julia Kelly,
Joe Kraynak, and Heather Williamson

HEWLETT-PACKARD CO.
Lake Stevens Library
8600 Soper Hill Road
Everett, WA 98205-1298

que®

A Division of Macmillan Computer Publishing
201 West 103rd St., Indianapolis, Indiana 46290 USA

©1998 by Que® Corporation

All rights reserved. No part of this book shall be reproduced, stored in a retrieval system, or transmitted by any means, electronic, mechanical, photo-
copying, recording, or otherwise, without written permission from the
publisher. No patent liability is assumed with respect to the use of the information contained herein. While every precaution has been taken in the prepa-
ration of this book, the publisher and author assume no responsibility for
errors or omissions. Neither is any liability assumed for damages resulting
from the use of the information contained herein. For information, address
Que Corporation, 201 W. 103rd Street, Indianapolis, IN 46290. You can reach
Que's direct sales line by calling 1-800-428-5331.

Library of Congress Catalog Card Number: 97-80985

International Standard Book Number: 0-7897-1585-6

99 98   8 7 6 5 4 3 2 1

Interpretation of the printing code: The rightmost double-digit number is the
year of the book's first printing; the rightmost single-digit number is the number of the book's printing. For example, a printing code of 98-1 shows that
this copy of the book was printed during the first printing of the book in
1998.

Printed in the United States of America

Publisher John Pierce

Executive Editor Karen Reinisch

Editorial Services Director Carla Hall

Managing Editor Thomas F. Hayes

Acquisitions Editor Don Essig

Product Director Melanie Palaisa

Production Editor Lori A. Lyons

Editor Julie A. McNamee

Editorial Assistant Jennifer L. Chisholm

Book Designer Kim Scott

Cover Designer Dan Armstrong

Indexer Tim Tate

Production Team Erin Danielson, Jenny Earhart, DiMonique Ford, Laura A.
Knox, Heather Stephenson

CONTENTS

Introduction ix

1 TOURING INTERNET EXPLORER 4.0   1

Understanding Internet Explorer 4.0 and the Internet 1
Starting Internet Explorer 2
Touring the Screen Layout 3
Exploring the Toolbar 4
Quitting Internet Explorer 5

2 NAVIGATING THE WORLD WIDE WEB   7

Going to a Web page 7
Exploring a Web Site 8
Revisiting Favorite Web Pages 11
Surfing the Web 13

3 SEARCHING THE WORLD WIDE WEB   15

Starting the Search 15
Using Search Engines 18
Searching by Category 19
Re-Examining Web Sites with the History Explorer 20

4 GETTING INFORMATION FROM THE WEB   23

Retrieving a File 23
Decompressing Software 24
Capturing a Picture 25
Copying a Link 27

**5 USING INTERNET EXPLORER FOR FTP
    DOWNLOADS   29**

An Introduction to FTP 29
Opening an FTP Site 30
Retrieving an FTP File 31

6   Viewing Web Pages Offline   34
Browsing Offline 34
Printing a Web Page 35
Saving a Web Page 37

7   Managing Your Information   39
Organizing Favorite Web Pages 39
Viewing Thumbnail Favorites 41
Using the Favorites Explorer 42
Saving Link Shortcuts and Using Quick Links 43

8   Customizing Internet Explorer 4.0   46
Personalizing Your Start Page 46
Selecting a New Start Page 47
Tailoring Your Web Page Display 48
Altering the Browser Fonts 49

9   Communicating with Email   52
Composing and Sending a Message 52
Getting and Replying to Messages 54
Attaching a File 56
Using Your Address Book 57

10   The Windows Address Book   59
Understanding Email Addresses 59
Internet Address Directories 61
Using the Windows Address Book 63
Importing Addresses 67

11   Email Maintenance   69
Sorting Your Email 69
Filtering Messages 71
Deleting Old Email Messages 73
Compacting Mail Folders 73
Configuring Your Email Options 74

12 **USING OUTLOOK EXPRESS WITH OUTLOOK 97** **75**

Introducing Outlook 97 75

Importing Message Folders 76

Importing Your Personal Address Book 77

13 **SUBSCRIBING TO NEWSGROUPS WITH OUTLOOK EXPRESS FOR NEWS** **79**

Configuring Your Server 79

Configuring Your Message Windows 82

Getting a List of Newsgroups 83

Sorting the Newsgroup List.. 84

Subscribing to Newsgroups 86

14 **WORKING WITH NEWSGROUP ARTICLES** **88**

Downloading Article Headers 88

Tagging Articles 90

Downloading Selected Messages 91

Opening Articles 92

Printing Articles 93

Threading Articles 94

Replying to a Newsgroup 95

Replying to the Original Author 97

15 **USING THE INTERNET SECURELY** **99**

Setting Your Security Level 99

Assigning Web Sites to a Security Zone 101

Understanding Security Certificates 102

Using Microsoft Wallet 104

16 **INTEGRATING THE WEB AND THE PC** **106**

Installing the Web Integrated Desktop 107

Elements of the Web Integrated Desktop 108

17 **THE ACTIVE DESKTOP AND YOUR PC** **113**

About the Active Desktop 113

Using Shortcut Icons on the Desktop 117

18 USING DESKTOP COMPONENTS   121

Viewing Desktop Components 121
Adding a Desktop Component 122
Customizing a Desktop Component 124
Updating Desktop Components 126
Hiding a Desktop Component 128
Removing a Desktop Component 128

19 MANAGING SUBSCRIPTIONS   130

What Are Subscriptions? 130
Subscribing to a Site 131
Customizing Subscription Settings 132
Downloading Subscriptions Now 137
Viewing a Changed Site 139
Deleting a Subscription 139

20 MANAGING CHANNELS   140

What Are Channels? 140
Using Channels 140
Using the Channel Guide 142
Subscribing to Channels 143
Updating Channels 146
Changing a Channel's Subscription Settings 147
Deleting a Channel 147

21 USING ADD-ONS AND PLUG-INS   149

Enhancing Your Web Browser's Capabilities 149
Popular Explorer Add-Ons 151
Popular Explorer Plug-Ins 155
Finding Add-Ons and Plug-Ins 155

22 USING ACTIVEX CONTROLS   157

Understanding ActiveX Controls 157
Popular ActiveX Controls 159
Where to Find ActiveX Controls 160

23 PRESENTING WITH NETSHOW **162**

Introducing NetShow 162
Downloading and Installing NetShow 163
Using Microsoft NetShow 163

24 CONFERENCING WITH NETMEETING **169**

Placing a Conference Call 169
Sending Messages with Chat 170
Incorporating the Whiteboard 172

25 BUILDING YOUR OWN WEB PAGE **174**

Starting FrontPage Express 174
Formatting Text 175
Adding Graphics 176
Saving Your Web Page 178
Quitting FrontPage Express 179

26 PUBLISHING YOUR WEB PAGE **180**

Dealing with the Preliminaries 180
Saving Your Page to a Web Server 182
Uploading Files to an FTP Server 185

A INSTALLING INTERNET EXPLORER 4.0 **188**

Index 191

We'd Like to Hear from You!

QUE Corporation has a long-standing reputation for high-quality books and products. To ensure your continued satisfaction, we also understand the importance of customer service and support.

Tech Support

If you need assistance with the information in this book, please access Macmillan Computer Publishing's online Knowledge Base at **http://www.superlibrary.com/general/support**. If you do not find the answer to your questions on our Web site, you may contact Macmillan Technical Support by phone at **317/581-3833** or via email at **support@mcp.com**.

Also be sure to visit Macmillan's Web resource center for all the latest information, enhancements, errata, downloads, and more. It's located at **http://www.mcp.com/**.

Orders, Catalogs, and Customer Service

To order other QUE or Macmillan Computer Publishing books, catalogs, or products, please contact our Customer Service Department at **800/858-7674** or fax us at **800/835-3202** (International Fax: 317/228-4400). Or visit our online bookstore at **http://www.mcp.com/**.

Comments and Suggestions

We want you to let us know what you like or dislike most about this book or other QUE products. Your comments will help us to continue publishing the best books available on computer topics in today's market. Send feedback to:

Melanie Palaisa
Product Development Specialist
Macmillan Publishing
201 West 103rd Street
Indianapolis, Indiana 46290 USA
email: **mpalaisa@mcp.com**

Please be sure to include the book's title and author as well as your name and phone or fax number. We will carefully review your comments and share them with the author. Please note that due to the high volume of mail we receive, we may not be able to reply to every message.

Thank you for choosing QUE!

INTRODUCTION

Welcome to the *10 Minute Guide to Internet Explorer 4.0*—a quick and easy reference for one of the world's most powerful communication programs. As the latest version of Microsoft's browser, Internet Explorer 4.0 brings you enhanced capabilities and control for making the most of the World Wide Web. This *10 Minute Guide* shows you how to use Internet Explorer 4.0 to browse the web, send and receive email, make presentations for the web, and even create and publish your own web page.

The World Wide Web is a very exciting environment that offers a wealth of information and tremendous potential for communication, and Internet Explorer 4.0 is a terrific, full-featured suite of programs that can enrich your business, as well as your personal life. The *10 Minute Guide to Internet Explorer 4.0* makes mastering the web and Internet Explorer itself a fun, hands-on adventure.

USING THIS BOOK

The *10 Minute Guide to Internet Explorer 4.0* consists of 26 lessons. Each lesson is designed to require no more than 10 minutes to complete. If you're just starting with Internet Explorer or web browsers in general, work through the first four lessons to familiarize yourself with the program. As you become more comfortable with Internet Explorer, feel free to skip around the book and focus on the lessons that interest you the most.

Several special elements are used throughout the book to highlight specific types of information:

 Timesaver Tip Helpful suggestions to get you working more efficiently.

Plain English   Nontechnical definitions of terms that may be unfamiliar to some readers.

Panic Button   Warnings of possible problems, and information on how to solve them.

Several of the book's other features are designed to make your learning faster and easier:

- Numbered steps provide precise instructions for commonly needed procedures.

- Menu commands, toolbar buttons, and dialog box options that you select are printed in blue for easy recognition.

- Text that you enter is **boldface and blue**.

- Messages that appear onscreen are **boldface**.

TRADEMARKS

All terms mentioned in this book that are known to be trademarks have been appropriately capitalized. Que cannot attest to the accuracy of this information. Use of a term in this book should not be regarded as affecting the validity of any trademark or service mark.

TOURING INTERNET EXPLORER 4.0

In this lesson, you learn what Internet Explorer 4.0 is, how to start the program, what the key screen areas are, how the toolbar buttons are used, and how to quit the program.

UNDERSTANDING INTERNET EXPLORER 4.0 AND THE INTERNET

Internet Explorer 4.0 is a suite of tightly integrated programs that connect you and your computer to the world of information available through the Internet and the World Wide Web. Internet Explorer not only acts as a browser to display the data, but it also helps you find, incorporate, and interact with that data. Internet Explorer also includes all the tools needed for you to communicate your message globally.

How does your computer communicate with the rest of the world? The necessary hardware is called a *modem* and is used to translate signals that come and go over the phone line. The necessary software for interpreting those signals into data that your computer can understand is known as a *browser*. Internet Explorer is the latest generation of Microsoft browser software.

Internet A group of computer networks from around the world that are connected to one another. Initially established to share text-based information between universities and research scientists, the Internet has evolved into a more open medium, accessible by everyone.

World Wide Web The Internet's graphic front end, accessed by browsers such as Internet Explorer.

After your hardware and software are set up to go onto the Internet, you need one final link: a connection to the Internet itself. If you are working in an office with a local area network, you may already be connected—check with your manager of information services or other computer consultant. If you are working at home or in a small office, you need to set up an account with an Internet service provider (ISP). Some ISPs, such as America Online, Microsoft Network (MSN), and CompuServe, provide additional, member-only services as well as Internet access. Other ISPs specialize in providing just the Internet connection. The choice is yours.

Starting Internet Explorer

Before you can start Internet Explorer, you must install the program on your computer. See installation instructions in Appendix A, "Installing Internet Explorer 4.0."

Depending on the type of Internet connection you have set up, you may need to connect to your ISP directly before starting Internet Explorer. Check with your ISP's technical support department.

Because of Internet Explorer's tight integration into the Windows 95 operating system, there are several ways to start the program. No matter how you have installed the program, you can always start Internet Explorer by following these steps:

1. From the Windows 95 taskbar, click the Start button.

2. From the Start menu, click Programs.

3. From the Programs submenu, click Internet Explorer found in the Internet Explorer Suite.

 Internet Explorer 4.0 Quick Start   On most Windows 95 desktops, you can double-click the Internet icon to start Internet Explorer.

If you are connected to the Internet, Internet Explorer opens your Start Page. Lesson 8, "Customizing Internet Explorer 4.0" tells you how to customize your Start Page.

TOURING THE SCREEN LAYOUT

Before you begin exploring the Internet and other capabilities of Internet Explorer, take a moment to familiarize yourself with the components of the screen. Table 1.1 describes the different sections of the screen and their uses, as shown in Figure 1.1.

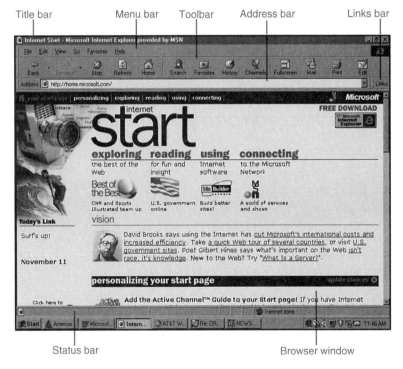

FIGURE 1.1   Sections of the Internet Explorer 4.0 screen.

TABLE 1.1   SECTIONS OF THE INTERNET EXPLORER 4.0 SCREEN

SCREEN ELEMENT	FUNCTION
Address bar	Displays current Internet address
Browser window	Primary display area
Links bar	Provides shortcuts to regularly updated web pages
Menu bar	Enables access to the Internet Explorer menu commands
Status bar	Displays information on connection status
Title bar	Displays program and current web page title
Toolbar	Provides shortcuts to basic program commands

 Customizing Toolbars   All the toolbars can be moved and resized with a simple click and drag on any bar area not covered by a button.

EXPLORING THE TOOLBAR

The shortcuts available in the toolbar across the top of Internet Explorer's screen go a long way toward simplifying your exploration of the World Wide Web. You'll find yourself returning to them time and again for both basic and more advanced operations. Here's a brief outline of the function of each toolbar button, from left to right across the screen:

- **Back** displays the previous web page.

- **Forward** returns to the most recent web page (if you have clicked the Back button).

- **Stop** interrupts the transfer of any web page from the Internet to your computer.

- **Refresh** reloads the current web page.

- **Home** opens the user-definable Start Page.

- **Search** opens a list of search engines used for finding a particular topic on the web.

- **Favorites** opens a list of your favorite web pages.

- **History** opens a list of the web pages you've visited, in reverse chronological order.

- **Channels** opens a list of currently available subjects you can subscribe to.

- **Fullscreen** expands the screen to its fullest size by temporarily hiding most of the toolbars and menus.

- **Mail** opens Internet Explorer's electronic mail and newsgroups menus.

- **Print** sends the current web page to your printer.

- **Edit** opens the current web page in the Internet Explorer editor, FrontPage Express, used for creating and updating web pages.

Web Page   A document created for the Internet that uses a particular protocol. This protocol, HTTP, enables web pages to link to one another and to convey not only text, but also multimedia sounds, graphics, and video.

Web Site   A collection of web pages.

QUITTING INTERNET EXPLORER

When you've finished your Internet Explorer session, you can quit the program by any of these standard methods:

- Select File, Exit from the menu bar.
- Click the Close button in the upper-right corner of the Internet Explorer window.
- Use the keyboard shortcut, Alt+F4.

In this lesson, you learned what Internet Explorer 4.0 is, how to start the program, what the key screen areas are, how the toolbar buttons are used, and how to exit the program. In the next lesson, you will learn how to navigate on the World Wide Web.

NAVIGATING THE WORLD WIDE WEB

*In this lesson, you learn how to go to a
specific web page, explore a web site, revisit favorite web pages, and
"surf" the web.*

GOING TO A WEB PAGE

When you begin to explore the Internet, you start by visiting
specific web pages. The web page address, or *URL*, could be given
to you by a friend or a colleague, or perhaps it is one you jotted
down from an advertisement or announcement.

**URL (Universal Resource Locator, pronounced "earl"
or "u-r-l")** A unique name used as an address by the
Internet. A URL begins with a protocol specification (such
as "http://"), followed by the specific web site name. The
last part of the URL designates the type of site; for instance, .com is for commercial, .edu is for educational
institutions, and .gov is for governmental agencies.

Internet Explorer, like all browsers, revolves around URLs. Finding, remembering, and managing these Internet addresses are a
lot of what Internet Explorer is about. Starting Internet Explorer
takes you to your first URL, the Internet Explorer Start Page. After
you are up and running, getting to a specific URL is easy.

Follow these steps to go to a specific web page:

1. Start Internet Explorer.

   The Internet Explorer Home Page is loaded. The status bar
   tells you what is happening. When the home page is
   completely loaded, the status bar displays **Done**.

2. Move the mouse pointer over the Address box. The pointer changes into an I-beam shape.

3. Click once anywhere in the Address box to select the current URL.

4. Type the URL. The first letter you type replaces the previous highlighted URL.

5. When you have completed typing the Internet address, press Enter.

   Internet Explorer connects to the requested web page.

Internet Explorer remembers URLs that you have visited. The next time you type in the address of a previously visited site, Internet Explorer automatically completes the address. Then you just press the Enter key to accept the completion and go to that web page.

TIP

More Auto-Completion   Most commercial URLs are variations of the http://www.company.com format. If you type just the main part of the web site address (the company part) and press Ctrl+Enter, Internet Explorer puts an "http://www." at the beginning and a ".com" at the end, and then connects to your requested site.

EXPLORING A WEB SITE

Few single web pages exist by themselves in cyberspace. Most are part of a larger structure called a web site. Because all web sites are designed independently, there is no common user interface among them. Most web sites open with a home page that contains *links* to other pages within their site.

Link   Short for a key concept on the World Wide Web: hypertext links. When a link is clicked, Internet Explorer opens that link, whether it is another web page (in the same or different site) or a downloadable graphic or sound.

Figure 2.1 shows a typical opening page for a web site. To explore a web site such as this one, follow these steps:

1. Go to a specific URL by typing an Internet address in the Address box and pressing Enter.

2. Move the pointer over the various elements of the page to identify the potential links:

   - Underlined words that are a different color from the rest of the text

   - Buttons or icons with clear directional signs

   - Graphic images, possibly surrounded by a border

   - Portions of a large graphic image

   When your mouse pointer passes over a link, the pointer changes to a hand.

3. Click once on any link to go to that web page.

4. If you want to return to the previous page, click the Back button in the toolbar.

5. If you see a link on the new page that interests you, click it to go to that page.

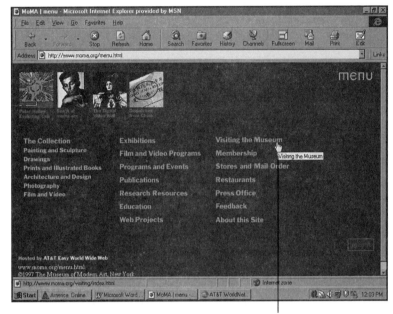

Mouse pointer

FIGURE 2.1   The mouse pointer changes to a hand to identify a link on the Museum of Modern Art's web site (www.moma.org).

Exploring a web site is a combination of following your nose and retracing your steps. Clicking links that lead from one page to another takes you down a particular path. Clicking the Back button on the toolbar brings you back the way you came, one page at a time.

Jump Back   If you right-click the Back button, a drop-down list of recently visited sites appears. You can jump to any listed URL by highlighting it with the mouse pointer and clicking once. The same is true of the *Forward button.*

REVISITING FAVORITE WEB PAGES

After a short time, you may want to revisit web sites that have valuable information you need to review or are updated frequently with new information. Internet Explorer enables you to mark any web page as a "Favorite" and to return there easily. Follow these steps to mark a web page as a Favorite:

1. Go to the web page you want to mark.

2. Click the Favorites button on the toolbar.

3. From the Favorites drop-down list, select Add to Favorites.

4. In the Add Favorite dialog box, Internet Explorer places the title of the web page in the Name text box. This is the name this page will be under in your Favorites list. If you want to, you can modify the page name by typing a new name in the box.

5. By default, Internet Explorer lists a new entry alphabetically in the Favorites folder. To list your selection in a different subfolder, click the Create In>> button.

6. The Add Favorite dialog box extends to display the available subfolders (see Figure 2.2):

   • To list the entry under an available folder, click that folder to open it.

   • To create a new folder, click the New Folder button and type in a new name. Press Enter.

7. The Add Favorite dialog box also handles web page subscriptions, discussed in Lesson 19, "Managing Subscriptions." Make sure the No, Just Add the Page to My Favorites option is selected.

8. Click OK.

FIGURE 2.2   You can easily add and categorize your Favorite
web pages.

You can accumulate a lot of Favorites over a short period of time,
and soon you'll find your Favorites drop-down list so long it can't
show all your choices. It's a good idea to organize your Favorites
as you add them. A standard Add Folder button in the extended
Add to Favorites dialog box enables you to create folders on-the-fly.

To access a web page that has been added to your Favorites collection, follow these steps:

1. Start Internet Explorer.

2. Click the Favorites button on the toolbar.

3. Highlight the desired web page or folder where the Favorite is stored, and click the Favorite name.

 Start Menu Favorites   If you installed the Integrated
Shell option, you'll find an additional category on the
Windows 95 Start menu after installing Internet Explorer:
Favorites. Click *Start*, then *Favorites*, and then any web
page you want to revisit. If Internet Explorer is not already
running, it will open and go directly to the requested web
page.

SURFING THE WEB

So, exactly how do you "surf" the web? The term comes from the practice of jumping from web page to web page by following the links available on various web sites. You can easily start out looking for information on animal vaccinations one minute and find yourself downloading audio clips from the Three Dog Night web site the next. That's part of the fun—and the distraction—of the Internet. Literally, everything is interconnected. Although all scenarios vary widely, follow these steps for a demonstration of how surfing the web can help your business:

1. Click in the Address box, type the URL for the Small Business Administration, **www.sbaonline.sba.gov**, and press Enter. Internet Explorer fills in the missing "http://".

2. From the SBA Home Page, use the scrollbar to move down the screen until you see the listing for Your Local SBA Resources and the multicolor map of the United States.

3. Click once on either the underlined words or the map image to jump to that page.

4. From the Local SBA Resources web page shown in Figure 2.3, click your regional area.

5. From the regional area map, click your state.

6. From the state map, click a city.

7. Select from the list of available SBA services, including loans, advice, and training.

8. Retrace your steps by clicking the Back button at any time.

Obviously, you can continue to follow any of the various paths to get the information you need. There is a vast amount of data on the web. Finding the right information requires a little patience, but can be gratifying, if not downright exciting.

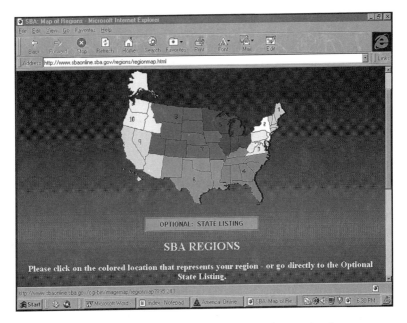

FIGURE 2.3   A web page that uses graphics for navigation.

 Business Research? To find more sites devoted to business issues, check out The *10 Minute Guide to Business Research* by Thomas Pack, published by Que.

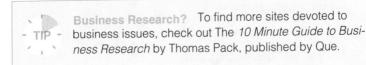 **Stopping a Web Page** If you encounter a web page that is taking forever to finish loading, click the *Stop* button on the toolbar. Pages load slowly either because of network delays or because the page has a lot of large graphic files.

In this lesson, you learned how to go to a specific web page, explore a web site, revisit favorite web pages, and "surf" the web. In the next lesson, you learn how to search the World Wide Web.

SEARCHING THE WORLD WIDE WEB

*In this lesson, you learn how to search
the Internet by using a search engine, how to search by category, and
how to set up your search page.*

STARTING THE SEARCH

The World Wide Web is made up of hundreds of thousands of
constantly changing web sites filled with vast amounts of data.
How can you find the information you need? Internet Explorer
4.0 gives you quick and easy access to a variety of different *search
engines* for this very purpose.

Search Engines Web sites devoted to cataloguing and
indexing the World Wide Web. When you submit a search
for keywords or a phrase, the search engine returns a list
of links to web pages that are relevant to your search.

Internet Explorer's innovative Search Explorer enables you to see
both the list of links returned by your search request and the web
pages connected to those links, as shown in Figure 3.1. With this
feature, you can quickly home in on your information without
having to constantly use the Back button.

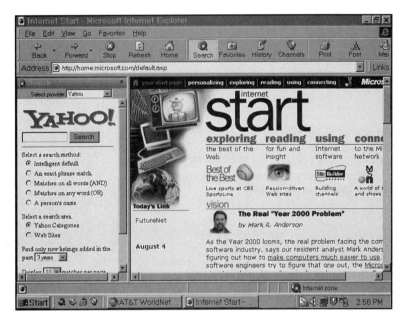

Figure 3.1 The Search Explorer lists available search engines.

To start a search, follow these steps:

1. Click the Search button on the toolbar. The Search toolbar opens in a frame on the left side of the screen.

2. In the Search box, type the keywords for your search.

3. If you would like to use a particular search engine, open the Select Provider drop-down list and choose a search engine. Currently supported search engines are:

   - **AltaVista (www.altavista.com)**   Indexes more web pages than most other services, but does not categorize them.

   - **Excite (www.excite.com)**   Searches by concept rather than keyword; Excite includes a directory of reviewed sites.

- **HotBot (www.hotbot.com)** Has fill-in-the-blank type boxes for selecting key search criteria such as keywords, dates, and places.

- **Infoseek (www.infoseek.com)** Categorizes and includes check marks next to sites that have been reviewed by the staff.

- **Lycos (www.lycos.com)** Uses WebGuides to highlight specific areas and continuously updates their Top 5% of the web list.

- **Yahoo! (www.yahoo.com)** Uses categories more extensively than the other services and includes special local search engines for metropolitan areas.

4. Click the Search button.

   A list of responses to your search query is returned in the left frame.

5. Move your mouse pointer over the resulting links. If available, a synopsis of the web page appears.

6. Select a link and click it.

   The selected web page appears in the right frame as shown in Figure 3.2.

7. To clear the search results and submit a new search, highlight the current keywords and type in your new keywords in the Search box.

8. To expand the right frame to full-screen, click the Search button.

Each search engine has its own style. Try them all to see which one suits you best.

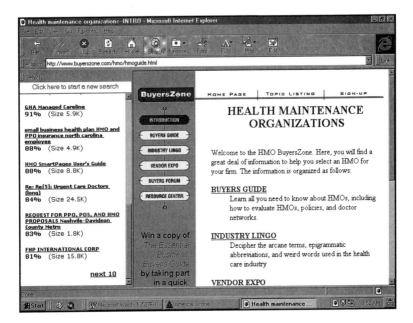

FIGURE 3.2   The search results on the left link to the web pages on the right.

USING SEARCH ENGINES

Submitting a single keyword for a search will likely result in thousands of responses. It's best to use multiple keywords to narrow your search. For example, "computer" will yield over 1.2 million responses; however, "computer technician LAN job NYC" returns only 23 responses. The opposite situation—restricting the search too tightly—can also be a problem. The phrase "travel magazines" returns far fewer results than "travel magazine" because the former searches only for those sites that indicate they work with multiple publications.

Follow these steps for better results in searching the web:

1. Click the Search button in the toolbar.

2. Use the following techniques in any combination to make your search more appropriate:

- **Multiple keywords**   Search engines look for documents with any of the words specified. Web pages that contain all the keywords are listed first. Example: computer technician LAN.

- **Double quotes**   Use double quotes around a phrase to look for the phrase and not the individual words. Example: "white house."

- **Plus sign (+)**   A plus sign in front of a word indicates that the word must be in the web page, but multiple words don't need to be necessarily together. Example: +OSHA requirements +CA.

- **Minus sign (-)**   A minus sign in front of a word indicates that the word must not be in the web page. Example: python antidote venom -monty.

- **Capitalization**   Enter all queries in lowercase unless a proper name is desired. Example: "White House."

3. Click Search.

All the search engines have advice for using the particular system better. Go to the search engine's home page and click pages labeled Tips or FAQ (Frequently Asked Questions).

Searching by Category

Sometimes, the best way to search for information is to start in a particular category and then enter your keywords. Most search engines are organized this way—Yahoo!, Lycos, Infoseek, and Excite among them. Searching by category also enables you to explore unanticipated avenues. Follow these steps to search by category:

1. In the Address bar, type the URL of any of the previously listed search engines.

2. Press Enter.

3. Click any highlighted category. Additional subcategories are listed at the top of the page before the pertinent web sites.

4. Follow the links through any additional subcategories to your desired topic.

> **TIP**
>
> **Favorite Categories** If you find a category page with a number of links that you want to reference, make it a Favorite for quick access. Lesson 2, "Navigating the World Wide Web," explains how to mark any page as a Favorite.

RE-EXAMINING WEB SITES WITH THE HISTORY EXPLORER

Quite often, you'll need to find a web site that you had previously visited. If you were at the web site earlier in the same session, you can right-click the Back button to choose from a drop-down list of recently visited sites. What if you were there yesterday or even two weeks ago? Internet Explorer has a new feature that enables you to keep track of—and link to—sites you visited up to three months ago.

The History button is part of the Explorer section on the toolbar, along with Search, Favorites, and Channels. Like those selections, clicking the History button opens a frame on the left side of the screen while keeping your current web page in a frame on the right. As you can see from Figure 3.3, the History frame divides the list of previously visited web sites by day.

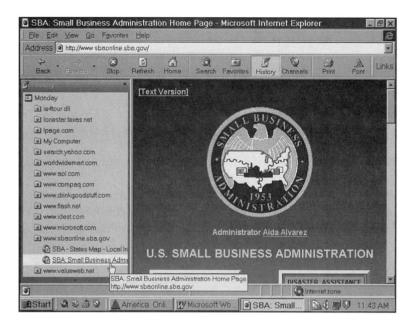

FIGURE 3.3   You can search your previous web site visits with the History feature.

To find a site you previously visited, follow these steps:

1. Click the History button on the toolbar.

2. Choose from one of the days listed in the History frame that opens on the right side of the screen. The day chosen expands to show a list of web sites visited on that day.

3. Click the individual web site to see a list of web pages you visited there.

4. Click any individual page to revisit it. Internet Explorer displays the selected web page in the right frame.

5. To close the History frame and expand the right frame to full-screen, click the History button.

Revising History   You can adjust how many days you want Internet Explorer to track your web-viewing history. From the View menu, choose Internet Options. On the General tab, change the value in the box next to Days to Keep Pages in History. The default setting is 20 days, but you can enter (or use the spinner controls) any value up to 99 days. You can also empty the History folder by clicking the Clear History button.

In this lesson, you learned how to search the Internet by using a search engine, how to search by category, and how to revisit web pages. In the next lesson, you learn how to download files and retrieve other information from the web.

GETTING INFORMATION FROM THE WEB

*In this lesson, you learn how to
retrieve a file, decompress downloaded software, capture a picture from
the web, and copy a link into your documents or onto the desktop.*

RETRIEVING A FILE

In addition to the vast amount of information available for
browsing on the web, there is also an enormous number of files
you can download. Graphics, software, compressed reports, and
entire books are just some of the types of files at hand.

 Downloading Transferring a file from a remote computer to your computer.

After you have downloaded a file, you can run it on your computer or incorporate it into your work. Internet Explorer 4.0 even
enables you to copy a link directly into an open document or
onto your desktop. Most files on the Internet intended to be
downloaded are clearly labeled. When you come across a file that
you want to download, follow these steps:

1. Click the link to the file to be downloaded.

2. Internet Explorer displays a system message telling you
   that you are about to download a file and warning you
   about viruses. Click Save to Disk and then click OK.

3. A Save As dialog box opens. If desired, choose a new place for the downloaded file to be saved by selecting a different folder or drive. Click OK. A Download File dialog box opens, as shown in Figure 4.1.

4. If necessary, you can click the Cancel button on the Download File dialog box to abort the transfer.

5. You can continue browsing the web or even quit Internet Explorer while the download is proceeding.

   After the file has finished downloading, the Download File dialog box closes.

Figure 4.1   A download in process.

 Easy File Recovery A good place to temporarily store your downloaded files is the Windows 95 desktop. An icon is created for your file that is easy to find. After you've finished with the file, you can drag it directly to the Recycle Bin.

Decompressing Software

Many downloadable files are compressed to reduce the file size and the download time. Software programs consisting of more than one file are compressed to keep all the separate files together. Some compressed files expand automatically when they are opened, but others require an outside application. The most popular compression scheme for Windows 95 is the ZIP method. Files that have been compressed by using this method have the extension .zip; these files are uncompressed with a program such as WinZip or PKZip. Before you can open a file with a .zip extension, you need to install one of these types of programs. You can find the programs in many places on the web. Two good sources for decompression programs are **www.tucows.com** and **www.shareware.com**.

Other files use a self-extracting method that automatically expands the file when it is opened; these files have an .exe or .sea extension. No special software is needed to open these files.

Follow these steps to decompress a downloaded file:

1. Locate the file that you have downloaded by opening its folder or by selecting Find File from the Start menu.

2. Double-click the icon for the file.

   The file opens with one of the following methods:

   - If the file has a .zip extension, the decompression program will open and decompress or extract the file.

   - If the file has an .exe or .sea extension, the file will open automatically and, if necessary, begin to install itself.

3. If the file has not automatically installed, open the file or folder created when the original download decompressed.

4. Load or install the program as necessary by double-clicking the icon.

CAPTURING A PICTURE

The graphics on the web can convey as much information as the text. You can capture almost any image that you see on the web and transfer it to your computer to view or use offline. Numerous sites are devoted to providing free clip art images. Be sure to check the copyright limitations on any web page before using someone else's work. To capture an image from the web, follow these steps:

1. Locate the image you want to copy.

2. Move the mouse pointer over the image and click the right mouse button.

3. From the Quick Menu, select Save Picture As, as shown in Figure 4.2.

4. From the Save As dialog box, choose a folder to save the image in and a new filename, if desired.

5. Click OK. The image copies to your computer.

Figure 4.2 shows an image in the process of being captured from the Flags of the World site at **http://flags.cesi.it/flags/**. Figure 4.3 shows the same image incorporated into the title page of a report written in Word 97.

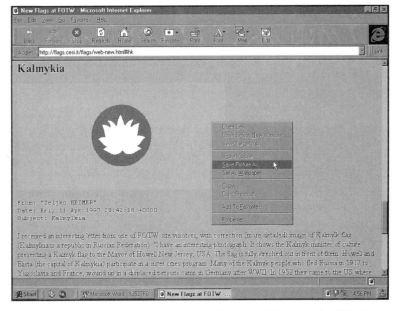

FIGURE 4.2   A flag image is copied from the Flags of the World web site.

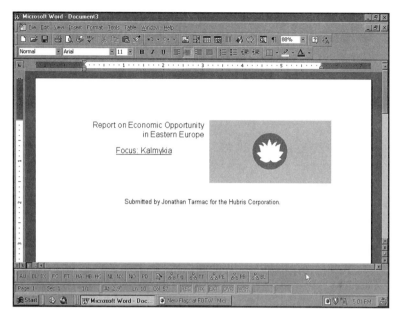

FIGURE 4.3   The same flag image is inserted into a Word document.

COPYING A LINK

As the modern world becomes increasingly tied into the World Wide Web, links to web pages are becoming more prevalent. Already, web page links can be on found on Desktops, in electronic mail, and in Office 97 documents. When you click these links, Internet Explorer starts, if it isn't already running, and opens the corresponding web site. Internet Explorer makes copying and using the links easy. Follow these steps to copy a link from any web page to the desktop:

1. Go to a web page that has a link you want to copy.

2. If Internet Explorer is maximized, click the Restore button in the title bar to reduce the Internet Explorer window.

3. Click and drag your desired link onto the desktop and release the mouse button. A shortcut to the web link is created on the desktop.

If you have Internet Explorer and another program such as Word 97 open side-by-side, you can click and drag the link directly into the program.

To copy a link from Internet Explorer to another program when they are not side-by-side, follow these steps:

1. Open a web page with the link you want to copy.

2. Position your pointer over the desired link.

3. Right-click the link to open the Quick menu.

4. From the Quick menu, select Copy Shortcut.

5. Switch to your other application by clicking its button in the taskbar.

6. Click the insertion point where you want the link to appear.

7. Click the Paste button in the toolbar. The link is copied to your program.

 Copy Not Linking? If you paste a link into Word 97 and - TIP - the text is there but it doesn't link, the AutoFormat option may be turned off. From the Tools menu, select AutoCorrect. Click the Autoformat As You Type tab and make sure there is a check mark in the Internet and Network Paths with Hyperlinks box.

In this lesson, you learned how to retrieve a file, how to decompress downloaded software, how to capture a picture from the web, and how to copy a link into your documents or onto the desktop. In the next lesson, you learn how to download software from FTP file servers.

Using Internet Explorer for FTP Downloads

In this lesson, you learn how to download files and other information directly from FTP sites by using Internet Explorer.

An Introduction to FTP

Although it's one of the oldest services on the Internet, FTP (File Transfer Protocol) is still one of the most popular services. FTP servers are strict file servers. They aren't connected to any other computers on the Internet, and you can connect to them only if you know their addresses. The sole purpose of an FTP server is to store files that other individuals can copy to their computers. Most FTP servers have thousands of files available for users to access.

FTP servers generally break users into two groups: members and guests. Because you must log on to every FTP site, you have to provide the computer with a name and password. If you are a member, the site manager provides this information. FTP site members generally get access to more information than the guests. If you are a guest, you can still access information, but it probably won't be everything on the server.

Guests generally log in as *anonymous*. On an anonymous FTP site, you can usually access services, but they ask one courtesy of you in return. Because you are an anonymous guest, most FTP sites ask you to use your full email address as a password. Although this takes away the opportunity for the user to work under total anonymity, it makes it easier for the FTP manager to track who is using the site and what types of files that person likes. The more information about the user that the site manager has access to, the better he or she can meet the needs of the user.

OPENING AN FTP SITE

Internet Explorer enables you to view FTP sites without any other software. There are several ways you can access these sites. The easiest is to select a link on a web page that connects to the FTP server. When you retrieve files from the Internet, you are often downloading them from FTP sites.

Another method you can use is to enter the address directly into Internet Explorer via either the Address field or the Open dialog box (shown in Figure 5.1). When you want to access an FTP site by using this method, you have to enter an **ftp://** in front of the address you are accessing. For example, if you want to open Microsoft's FTP site (**ftp.microsoft.com**), you type **ftp:// ftp.microsoft.com**.

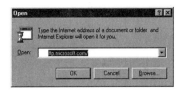

FIGURE 5.1   Internet Explorer enables you to open an FTP site from its Open dialog box.

Need a Prefix You don't have to type the prefix ftp://. Internet Explorer understands that any site address beginning with ftp is an FTP site, and it configures itself accordingly.

RETRIEVING AN **FTP** FILE

FTP servers make thousands of files available to you on thousands of computers throughout the Internet. Most of these files are shareware or freeware programs, graphics, software applications, or informational files you can download. You often need to download a file, but you might not have access to an FTP client. Internet Explorer provides you with an immediate way to access those files.

Although there are files on FTP servers that are readable only by Macintosh or UNIX machines, there are plenty available for your Windows machine. Follow these steps to download a file from an FTP site:

1. Open Macmillan Computer Publishing's FTP site by entering the URL **ftp://ftp.mcp.com/** in either the Address box or the Open dialog box. When this site opens (see Figure 5.2), you see the list of files at the root directory of Macmillan Computer Publishing's site.

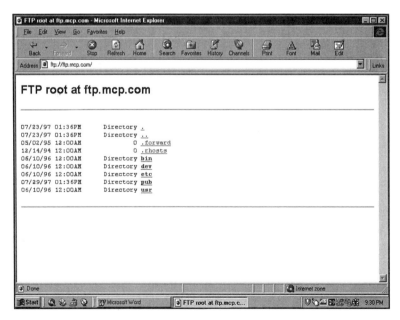

FIGURE 5.2   You can search Macmillan's archives for software.

Index.txt   Well-organized FTP sites provide an index file you can use to easily locate the file you're looking for. With this file at your fingertips, you don't have to worry about guessing which file is the right one for you or downloading the wrong file.

2. Select the pub link. This opens a list of the files in the /pub/ directory. To continue to download the software file, click the software link.

3. Click Windows 95.

4. To download the htmlasst.zip file, click its link. The Internet Explorer File Download Wizard starts to copy the file from the FTP server onto your computer (see Figure 5.3).

Figure 5.3   The File Download Wizard controls all your download operations.

5. Click OK. Then select your Temp directory in which to store the file and click Save.

6. When the file is completely downloaded, click OK.

Downloading an FTP file is just like downloading a file from a web page. Simply click the file name and tell Internet Explorer where to save the file. After the file is downloaded, you can extract and install it by double-clicking its filename in Windows Explorer.

Almost all major software companies have an FTP site for product updates. Companies such as Symantec and McAfee use their FTP sites for distributing new virus lists for their anti-virus programs. New software is often put into an FTP site for downloading before it is made available on the web. You can be the envy of your office when you own the newest copy of Internet Explorer before your coworkers can even find it on the web!

In this lesson, you learned how to use Internet Explorer as an FTP file retrieval client. In the next lesson, you learn how to view web pages offline.

VIEWING WEB PAGES OFFLINE

In this lesson, you learn how to browse offline, print a web page, and save a web page.

BROWSING OFFLINE

It may seem that there is so much on the web that you have to stay connected to it 24 hours a day; but that's not the way people work. You work the web to access your research, contacts, and email—and then you go offline for most of the day. Internet Explorer 4.0 combines the best of both worlds with a new feature that enables you to browse your favorite sites offline. Follow these steps to browse web pages offline:

1. Go to a web page that you want to browse offline.

2. From the Favorites menu, select Add to Favorites.

3. From the Add Favorite dialog box, specify a new folder to save it in or rename the page if desired.

4. Click OK.

5. From the File menu, select Work Offline, as shown in Figure 6.1.

6. From the Favorites menu, highlight the web page you added to the Favorites collection. The web page appears, complete with any active content, as if you were online.

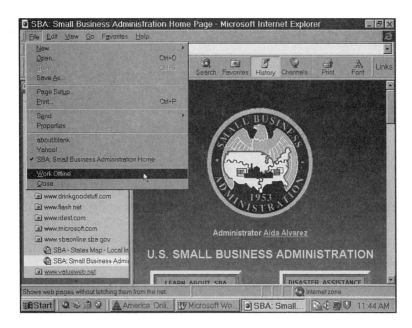

FIGURE 6.1   The Work Offline option is found under the File menu.

Browsing Offline Off?   If you keep getting the message that the page you requested is not available offline, the amount of file space reserved for temporary files may be set too low. From the View menu, click Internet Options. On the General tab, in the Temporary Internet files section, click Settings. Increase the Amount of Disk Space to Use by clicking and dragging the slider. Click OK here and in the Options dialog box.

PRINTING A WEB PAGE

Being able to get a printout of your data—no matter what the source—is vital to anyone in business. Today, much of the data gathered is from the web. Printing and saving web pages is extremely helpful if you are gathering sales research, making a presentation at an off-site meeting, or burning the midnight oil putting together a proposal. Printing a web page gives you instant hands-on access. Follow these steps to print a web page:

1. Browse to the web page you want to print.

2. From the File menu, choose Print. The Print dialog box opens as shown in Figure 6.2.

3. Select from the following options:

   - **Print Range**   Because web pages do not correspond one-to-one to printed pages, it's best to leave the Print All box selected.

   - **Copies**   Type the number of copies you want or use the incrementer arrows to print more than one.

   - **Linked Documents Checking**   Print all Linked Documents makes Internet Explorer download and print any web page with a direct link to the current page.

   - **Print Table of Links**   Clicking this option enables you to see a list of what pages are linked to the current one.

   - **Print Frames**   These options activate when the page in question contains frames. You can print a portion of a screen by clicking in one frame and selecting Only the Selected Frame.

4. Click **OK**.

TIP   **Wrong-Way Printing**   Because the web is a screen-based medium instead of a page-based one, some web pages look better printed horizontally instead of vertically. To change the page orientation, select Page Setup from the File menu. In the Page Setup dialog box, choose either Portrait (the default, vertical) or Landscape (horizontal) in the Orientation section.

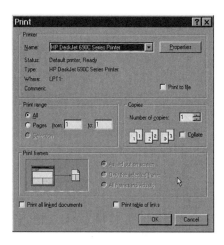

FIGURE 6.2   The Print dialog box with special web page options.

SAVING A WEB PAGE

If you need to incorporate data you found on the web into a report or other document, browsing offline and printing the page doesn't do the trick. For times like these, you need to be able to save the web page to your computer's hard drive. Internet Explorer enables you to save web pages in two ways: as a text file and as an HTML file. Save your web pages in .txt format when you want just the text. An HTML file includes the web page layout as well as the text as it appears on the web. Although saved HTML files show spaces for the graphics, they don't automatically save the images (to save a web graphic, see the "Capturing a Picture" section in Lesson 4).

HTML (Hypertext Markup Language)   HTML is the computer language used to build web pages. HTML files end with either an .htm or .html extension.

To save a web page, follow these steps:

1. Browse to a web page that you want to save to disk.

2. From the File menu, select Save As.

3. From the Save HTML Document dialog box, enter a new folder to save the file in, if desired.

4. Select a file type option by clicking the arrow next to the Save as Type box as shown in Figure 6.3:

   - **HTML file** (*.htm, *.html) saves as HTML files.

   - **Text file** (*.txt) saves as a text file.

5. Type a new filename in the File Name box.

6. Click OK.

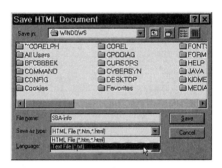

Figure 6.3   The Save HTML Document dialog box showing available file types.

In this lesson, you learned how to browse offline, how to print a web page, and how to save a web page. In the next lesson, you learn how to manage your web information.

MANAGING YOUR INFORMATION

*In this lesson, you learn to organize
your favorite web pages, view thumbnails of your Favorites, and use
Favorite Explorer, Link Shortcuts, and Quick Links.*

ORGANIZING FAVORITE WEB PAGES

After you get into the habit of adding web pages to your list of
Favorites, it's hard to stop. Soon your list extends to the bottom
of your screen, and remembering why you selected every entry is
next to impossible. It's time to organize your favorite web pages.
Internet Explorer 4.0, like Windows 95, uses folders as a primary
organizational aid. Folders take up almost no physical hard drive
space, and they can help you find your files more quickly while
avoiding clutter. Internet Explorer provides the Organize Favorites
dialog box for arranging your favorite web pages.

Follow these steps to organize your favorite web pages:

1. From the Favorites menu, select Organize Favorites.

2. The Organize Favorites dialog box opens, as shown in
   Figure 7.1, and displays the folders and web sites selected
   in Internet Explorer. If you installed the Integrated Shell,
   Favorites selected in other Office 97 programs such as
   Word 97 are displayed as well.

3. When the Organize Favorites dialog box opens, all the
   command buttons, with the exception of the Close button, are inactive. Click any file or folder to activate the
   buttons.

4. From the Organize Favorites dialog box, select any of the following options:

- **Move**   Opens the Browse for Folder dialog box to display all folders in your Favorites collection. Click any folder to move the selected file there. Click OK.

- **Rename**   Highlights the name of the selected file or folder. Type in a new name and press the Enter key.

- **Delete**   Places the selected file or folder in the Recycle Bin. Before proceeding, Internet Explorer asks for confirmation. From the Confirm File Delete dialog box, choose Yes to delete, No to cancel.

- **Open**   Opens the selected file or folder. This is useful if you don't remember what the Favorite is.

5. To create a new folder, click the New Folder button in the dialog box toolbar. Enter the new folder name and press Enter.

6. When you have finished organizing your Favorites, click OK to close the dialog box.

FIGURE 7.1   The Organize Favorites dialog box arranges all your selected web sites.

Dragging Favorites   You can move your Favorites around by clicking and dragging them both in the Organize Favorites dialog box and on the Favorites menu. Just click the Favorite you want to move, drag it onto a folder, and release the mouse button.

VIEWING THUMBNAIL FAVORITES

After you have organized your Favorites, you still might have trouble remembering what each filename means. If you installed the Integrated Shell, Internet Explorer provides a visual alternative to often cryptic filenames: thumbnails. Thumbnails are basically small pictures used as reminders.

To view your Favorites as thumbnails, follow these steps:

1. Click in the Address bar and type c:\windows\ favorites.

2. Press Enter. Your Favorites are displayed in the browser window.

3. From the View menu, select Thumbnails.

   The view switches to Thumbnail view (with a Windows Explorer toolbar) as shown in Figure 7.2.

4. To go to any Favorite shown, double-click the thumbnail.

5. To return to your previous Internet Explorer page, click the Back button in the toolbar.

Thumbnails for Other Folders   You can display what's inside other folders besides the Favorites folder. Select a folder you want to display and right-click to reveal the Quick Menu. From the Quick Menu, select Properties. From the Properties dialog box, on the General tab, check Enable Thumbnail View.

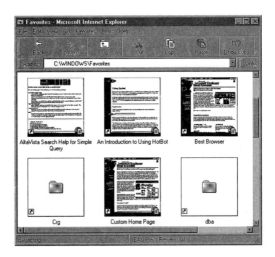

FIGURE 7.2   A Sample Thumbnail view shows both web pages and folders.

USING THE FAVORITES EXPLORER

In addition to accessing your web site Favorites through the menu, you can also use the split window Explorer feature. Just like the Search, History, and Channel buttons, clicking the Favorites button on the toolbar opens a frame on the left side of the screen to display a list while keeping web pages visible in the frame on the right. Using the Favorites Explorer enables you to quickly review your current selections so you can print, rename, or delete them.

To use the Favorites Explorer, follow these steps:

1. Click the Favorites button on the toolbar. The screen splits into two frames, as shown in Figure 7.3. The frame on the left contains a listing of your Favorites. The currently selected web site is in the frame on the right.

2. To go to a web page Favorite, click the page name. The web page opens in the right frame.

3. To look inside a folder, highlight the folder and click it. The web pages in the folder are displayed in an indented list.

4. Right-click the Favorite when you want to print, rename, or delete it. Choose your action from the Quick menu that appears.

5. To close the Favorites frame and expand the right frame to full-screen, click the Favorites button.

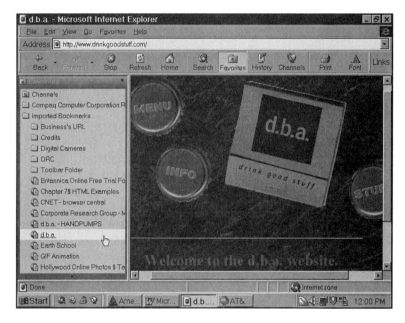

FIGURE 7.3   Explore your collection of favorite web pages through the split-screen Favorites feature.

SAVING LINK SHORTCUTS AND USING QUICK LINKS

Those web sites you access the most frequently can be set up for one-click access from the desktop or from the Links toolbar.

Although the Favorites menu is convenient for most revisits to web pages, there are times when you want to go to a site again and again; you might need to look up a zip code often or keep in touch with a competitor's web site. Internet Explorer has two features for these circumstances: Link Shortcuts and Quick Links. A shortcut is an icon that acts as a pointer to a program or, in this case, a link to a web page. Shortcuts are usually found on the Windows 95 desktop, although they can exist in any folder.

To create a shortcut to a link, follow these steps:

1. Go to the web page containing the link to which you want to create a shortcut.

2. If your Internet Explorer screen is maximized, click the Restore button in the title bar.

3. Click the link you want, drag it to the desktop, and release the mouse button. A Link Shortcut is created on the desktop.

To access your web page via the Link Shortcut, double-click the desktop shortcut. If Internet Explorer is open, the web page loads; if not, Internet Explorer opens and then loads the web page.

 TIP   **Flipping to the Desktop**   If you have the Desktop Integration mode turned on, you can bring the desktop to the front just as you would any open window. Click the Surface/Restore Desktop icon on the right side of the taskbar.

A Quick Link is a user-specified button on the Links toolbar. Internet Explorer has room for up to five Quick Links. To connect a web site to a Quick Link button, follow these steps:

1. Go to the web site containing the link you want to make into a Quick Link.

2. If the Links toolbar is not fully visible, click the word Links.

3. Click your desired link, drag it up to any of the other buttons on the Links toolbar, and release the mouse button.

   The Quick Link dialog box opens, as shown in Figure 7.4.

4. From the Quick Link dialog box, click Yes to set the Quick Link to the selected web address or click No to cancel.

5. If you clicked Yes, the name of the Quick Link button changes to your selected site.

6. Click the Quick Link button to load the chosen web page.

7. Click the word Links to shrink the Links toolbar.

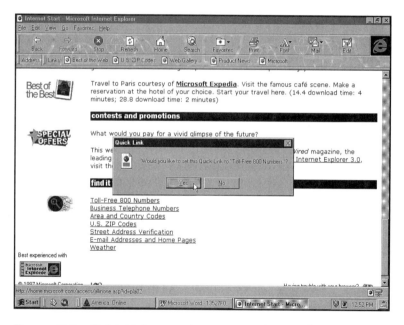

FIGURE 7.4 Quick Links can give you a custom toolbar.

In this lesson, you learned how to organize your favorite web pages, view thumbnails of your Favorites, and use Favorite Explorer, Link Shortcuts, and Quick Links. In the next lesson, you learn how to customize Internet Explorer.

LESSON 8

CUSTOMIZING INTERNET EXPLORER 4.0

In this lesson, you learn how to personalize your Start Page, select a different Start Page, customize your general web page settings, and choose a different font size for web pages.

PERSONALIZING YOUR START PAGE

Every time Internet Explorer opens, it goes to its Start Page. The default Start Page is maintained by Microsoft and offers an excellent entry into the Internet. One advantage that this page has over others is that you can get daily headlines (and their links) in a variety of categories. You also get to choose the categories and the content providers used. For example, you could pick the Sports and Stock Ticker categories or you could opt for Technology, Money, and Entertainment categories. Follow these steps to personalize the Internet Explorer Start Page:

1. Start Internet Explorer.

2. From the Microsoft Start Page, click the Personalizing button located at the top of the web page.

3. From the Personalizing page shown in Figure 8.1, click the category under step 1 that you want to alter.

4. For each category, different options appear under step 2. Select any desired option by clicking its logo's check box.

5. To step through the categories one at a time, click the Next button under step 3.

6. When you have made all your choices, click the Finish button under step 3.

   Your Start Page is reloaded with your new options enabled.

FIGURE 8.1 Personalizing your Start Page to give you the headlines you want.

Stock Ticker Delay The Stock Ticker option needs a small program called an ActiveX control to run on your Start Page. After you have clicked the Finish button, the ActiveX control downloads and installs into your system. This may take several minutes.

SELECTING A NEW START PAGE

There are some circumstances when you might want to choose an entirely different Start Page. If your business has its own web site, you might prefer using that home page as your starting point. Or, you might have a news source specific to your industry that is not available through Microsoft. Internet Explorer enables you to choose your own Start Page as well as your own Search and Quick

Link pages, covered in Lesson 7. To select a web site as your new Start Page, follow these steps:

1. Go to the web page that you want to set up as your Start Page.

2. From the View menu, select Internet Options.

3. Click the General tab.

4. In the Home page section, click the Use Current button. The current URL appears in the Address box.

5. Click OK.

TAILORING YOUR WEB PAGE DISPLAY

If you enter a web site with intensive graphics and multimedia elements, the World Wide Web can become the World Wide Wait. Internet Explorer enables you to turn off certain elements to speed up the downloading of web pages. You can independently control pictures, sounds, and videos with Internet Explorer. Internet Explorer also enables you to customize the colors of your web browser. Many web pages, particularly the text-intensive ones, use the browser defaults when displaying background, text, and link colors. Use this feature to reduce eyestrain or increase the contrast between text and background.

To alter your web browser's display, follow these steps:

1. From the View menu, select Internet Options. The Options dialog box appears.

2. From the Advanced tab, remove the check mark next to the multimedia elements to stop the pictures, sounds, or videos from automatically displaying (see Figure 8.2). Click again to enable them.

3. To change the colors, click the Colors button on the General tab.

4. From the Colors dialog box, click Use Windows Colors to deselect it.

5. Click the box next to Background to open the Color Picker dialog box.

6. Click a desired color, and then click OK.

7. Repeat steps 4 – 6 to choose the text color.

8. You can follow the same procedure to alter either of the Visited or Unvisited Link colors. If you click the Use Hover Color box, text links change to the specified color when your mouse passes over them.

9. Click OK.

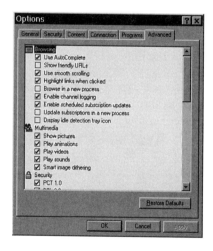

FIGURE 8.2   Customizing your web browser with the Options dialog box.

ALTERING THE BROWSER FONTS

With Internet Explorer, you can alter the size of the font normally used to display web page text. This is useful when you need to make the text larger for presentation purposes or smaller to see more on a page. These changes are also reflected in any printouts of the page. You can either alter the font size temporarily or specify your new size as the default. To temporarily alter the size of the default font, follow these steps:

1. From the View menu, select Internet Options. The Options dialog box appears.

2. From the General tab, click the Fonts button

3. Select one of the five available sizes ranging from Largest to Smallest. Medium is the default.

4. Open a web page to see the resulting changes.

5. To make your new font size the default, click the Set as Default button.

Unless you've made it the default, the new font size stays in effect until you change it using the preceding method or until you close Internet Explorer. Figure 8.3 shows the same web page using the smallest and the largest available fonts.

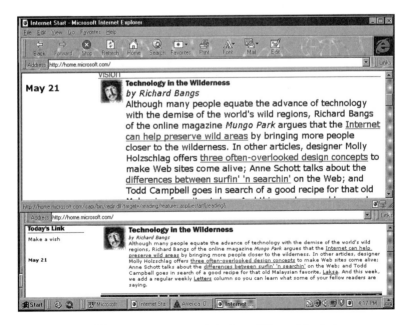

FIGURE 8.3   The same paragraph in two different font sizes.

In this lesson, you learned how to personalize your Start Page, select a different Start Page, customize your general web page settings, and choose a different font size for web pages. In the next lesson, you learn how to use email.

9 COMMUNICATING WITH EMAIL

In this lesson, you learn how to compose and send a message, reply to and forward email you receive, attach a file, and use your Address Book.

COMPOSING AND SENDING A MESSAGE

Email in the '90s is becoming what faxes were in the '80s: indispensable. For worldwide business, interoffice and even personal communication, electronic mail is fast, inexpensive, and convenient. Internet Explorer 4.0 includes a powerful email component called Outlook Express that makes sending all forms of electronic communication—notes, documents, graphics, and even multimedia files—a breeze.

To compose and send email to anyone on the Internet, follow these steps:

1. If it is not already running, start Internet Explorer.

2. Click the Mail icon in the toolbar.

3. From the drop-down option list, click New Message. The New Message form opens as shown in Figure 9.1.

Insert File button

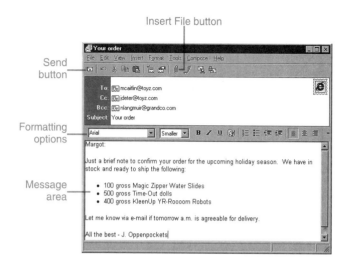

Send button

Formatting options

Message area

FIGURE 9.1 The New Mail form, filled out and ready to send.

4. Type the recipient's email address in the To box—for example, **jsmith@smithco.com**.

5. Press Tab to move to the next box.

6. Enter any additional recipients in the Cc and Bcc boxes and press Tab.

7. In the Subject box, type in your email message title and press Tab.

8. Type your text in the message area. You can use any of the formatting options available in the toolbar above the message area, including bold, italic, underline, font (name, color, and size), alignment, and bulleted or numbered lists.

9. To put your email into the Outbox, click the Send button (the envelope) in the Outlook Express toolbar.

10. Outlook Express asks if you want to send your email now. Click Yes or No.

TIP **Sending Unsent Mail** Unsent email goes into the Outlook Express Outbox. Click the Mail button and select Read Mail to open Outlook Express. Click the Outbox folder in the left pane. Select the email to send and click the Send and Retrieve button on the toolbar.

GETTING AND REPLYING TO MESSAGES

After you open up your email box, you'll be amazed at the number of messages you receive. It's best to respond quickly to your email, as with any communication. Internet Explorer makes replying easy and offers a number of other options for email handling as well. First, you need to know how to get your mail.

To retrieve your mail, follow these steps:

1. From the Internet Explorer toolbar, click the Mail button.

2. From the drop-down list, select Read Mail to open Outlook Express.

3. From the Outlook Express Tools menu, select Retrieve.

4. From the submenu, select All Accounts or a single account.

   Any mail received goes into the Inbox. The number of new messages appears in parentheses next to the Inbox in the Folder List, as shown in Figure 9.2.

5. To read a message, select it from the Message List. The message opens in the Preview Pane.

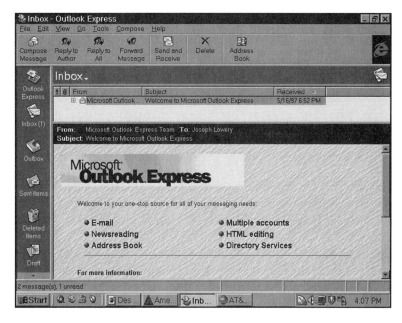

FIGURE 9.2   Outlook Express displays messages in the Preview Pane.

To respond to an email message, follow these steps:

1. Open Outlook Express, if it isn't already running.

2. From the Message List, click the message you want to respond to.

3. Click the Reply to Author button on the toolbar.

   The Reply form opens with the To and Subject boxes filled in. The insertion pointer is in the message area.

4. Type your reply.

5. Click the Send button in the Reply form toolbar.

Repeating Messages? By default, Outlook Express includes the original message after your reply. To disable this feature, select Mail Options from the Tools menu. On the Send tab, uncheck Include Message in Reply. Click OK.

ATTACHING A FILE

One of email's most powerful features is its capability to attach any document to your message. This feature has greatly enhanced productivity between working groups by enabling them to share files across the office or the country. Word processing documents, spreadsheets, or graphics all can be sent with equal ease. You only have to be certain that whoever is receiving the files has the capability (or software) to view them.

To attach a file to your email, follow these steps:

1. Compose a new message or respond to a previous message.

2. From the Message toolbar, click the Insert File button. The Insert Attachment dialog box appears.

3. From the Insert Attachment dialog box, select a file and click OK.

4. An icon for the file appears in a box below the message area, as shown in Figure 9.3. To send additional attachments, repeat steps 2–4.

5. Click the Send button to send the email message with the attachments.

When the email is sent, your message is sent first and then the attached file or files are uploaded. The time it takes to send the entire email message and attachments depends on the size of the files and the speed of the Internet connection.

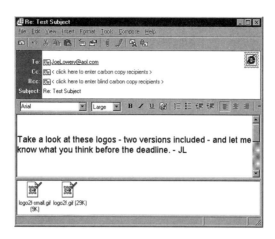

FIGURE 9.3   An email reply with attachments.

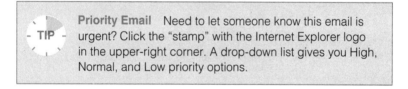

Priority Email   Need to let someone know this email is urgent? Click the "stamp" with the Internet Explorer logo in the upper-right corner. A drop-down list gives you High, Normal, and Low priority options.

USING YOUR ADDRESS BOOK

The Address Book is a key component of any email system. Internet Explorer and Outlook Express use the central Windows Address Book found in Outlook and all Office 97 applications. With Internet Explorer, the Address Book's major emphasis is on email addresses—the often cryptic, hard-to-remember strings of characters that take the form **jsmith@somewhere.com**.

Follow these steps to send an email message to someone in your Address Book:

1. Click the Mail button in the Internet Explorer toolbar and then select New Mail from the drop-down list.

2. From the New Mail form, click the Address Book icon (the rolodex card) next to the To box. The Select Recipients dialog box opens, as shown in Figure 9.4.

3. From the Name List on the left, double-click the name of the intended recipient. The name appears in the To box.

4. To add additional recipients, repeat steps 3 and 4.

5. Click OK.

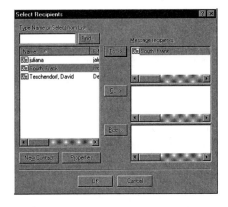

FIGURE 9.4 The Address Box maintains a list of all your contacts through the Select Recipients dialog box.

In this lesson, you learned how to compose and send a message, reply to and forward email you receive, attach a file, and use your Address Book. In the next lesson, you learn more details about working with the Windows Address Book.

THE WINDOWS ADDRESS BOOK

LESSON 10

In this lesson, you learn how to use the Windows Address Book with Outlook Express for storing and managing your email addresses.

UNDERSTANDING EMAIL ADDRESSES

Email addresses are often used as an individual's personal identifier on the Internet. They enable users to send and receive information all across the Internet. An email address serves as a phone number, but instead of identifying a particular house, it identifies a particular person or company. Email addresses use a variety of formats depending upon the network that you're using, but Internet email addresses follow one main form.

A typical email address consists of two distinct parts. The first part identifies a unique user (userid) on the network, and the second identifies the specific system (host) that user belongs to. On some networks, userids are case sensitive. On these systems jack, Jack, and JACK are three separate userids or individuals. The Internet uses a system of *Domain Name* specifications to track specific hosts and their classifications. Table 10.1 shows you the main top-level domains, or extensions, that are available.

 Domain Names Every computer has its own address on the Internet that other computers use to find it. These addresses are used to identify the computers and networks that are permanently attached to the Internet. Your personal computer does not have a domain name because you connect through your service provider, who does have a domain name.

TABLE 10.1   EMAIL ADDRESS EXTENSIONS AND THEIR INTENDED ORIGINS

EXTENSION	ORIGIN
edu	Universities, colleges, all school systems
com	Commercial businesses
mil	Military bases and organizations
gov	Government agencies
org	Organizations
net	Networking units such as Internet service providers

Most host systems outside the United States tend to be registered under both a country code and a domain extension. Although this is a good rule of thumb, hostnames aren't always indicative of their source or geographic location. A good example of this is microsoft.com, which is composed of a series of hosts located throughout the world, not just in the United States.

Many different computers or networks are registered under a specific domain. For example, suppose that a company has the domain catsback.com. This would indicate that the company is a commercial business organization. The company would then be responsible for managing any other hostnames that fall within its domain. For example, **www.catsback.com** might represent the computer hosting Cat's Back's web site, just as the address **ftp.catsback.com** would represent the computer hosting its FTP archives. And, as you might guess, **mail.catsback.com** would be the name of the company's mail server.

Internet email addresses consist of a userid followed by an ampersand and the hostname, so you create an address similar to **userid@computer.subdomain.domain**. Following this model, an email address for this company could be **catsback@mail.catsback.com**. Because there's no limit to the size of an address, an individual could have an address resembling this: **jaque_b_tourlebouland@otime.cntrinvbur.ak-dpt.staterept.paris.mil.fr**.

INTERNET ADDRESS DIRECTORIES

A wide variety of internationally accessible email address books located on the Internet. By using these LDAP (Lightweight Directory Access Protocol) email address books, you can quickly and effortlessly add the addresses that you find to your Windows Address Book.

 LDAP   The Lightweight Directory Access Protocol was originally designed as an Internet client server protocol for accessing the preexisting X.500 directory services. Since its origination, LDAP has evolved to become a standard means of accessing online directory systems.

Outlook Express provides you with immediate access to the most popular LDAP directories. These directories include: Four11 (**http://www.four11.com**), Switchboard (**http://www.swithcom**), InfoSpace (**http://www.infospace.com**), BigFoot (**http://www.bigfoot.com**), and Who/Where (**http://www.whowhere.com**).

When you need to look up an individual on these systems, you can use the following steps:

1. Open the Start menu, select Programs, and then Windows Address Book. If you already have Outlook Express running, you can click the Address Book button, or you can open the Tools menu and select Address Book (Ctrl+Shift+B).

2. Click the Find button, or open the Edit menu and select Find (Ctrl+F).

3. Select the directory service that you want to use from the Search list (see Figure 10.1).

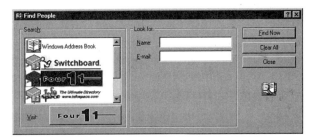

FIGURE 10.1   The Find People dialog box enables you to search both your local address book and a variety of Internet directories.

4. Enter the information that you want to search for, whether it is a user's name, email address, postal mail address, or phone number in your local address book. If you have selected one of the Directory services, enter either a name or email address.

5. Click the Find Now button.

6. If the individual that you're looking for is listed with that service, her name appears in the search results window shown in Figure 10.2.

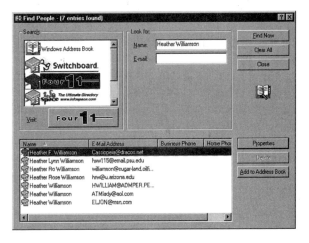

FIGURE 10.2   The results of your search are displayed for you.

7. Select the name that you want to add to your address book, and then click Add to Address Book.

8. Click Close.

USING THE WINDOWS ADDRESS BOOK

The Windows Address Book places everything at the tip of your fingers. You have access to all its key features directly from the main toolbar. With the click of a button, you can add a new contact to your local address book, edit an existing contact, or simply group some of the contacts you already have.

ADDING A CONTACT

To create a new address book entry, follow these steps:

1. Open the Start menu, select Programs, and then Windows Address Book. If you already have Outlook Express running, you can click the Address Book button, or you can open the Tools menu and select Address Book (Ctrl+Shift+B).

2. Click the New Contact button, or open the File menu and select New Contact (Ctrl+N).

3. Enter the individual's first, middle, and last name in the appropriate fields (see Figure 10.3). These names are combined to create an automatic display name. You also can choose to fill in a nickname for the individual you're adding.

4. In the E-Mail Addresses section, click the Add New field and type in the full address you want to use, such as **jack@whitehouse.gov**.

5. Click the Add button.

6. If you want to send only plain text messages to these individuals, check the Send E-Mail Using Plain Text Only check box at the bottom of the screen.

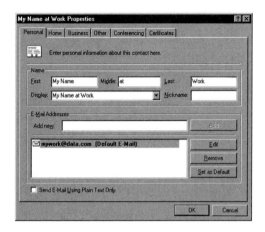

FIGURE 10.3 The Properties dialog box, from which you can add a New Contact.

7. Click the Home tab. On this tab you can store the personal mailing information about your contact. Included on this page is space for the individual's Personal Web Page address. Be sure to leave **http://** attached to the front of the page address.

8. Click the Business tab. This screen enables you to store all the business information for your contact, including an address for his or her business web site.

9. Click the Other tab, and you can store notes about this particular individual.

10. Click the NetMeeting tab. If you have installed Microsoft NetMeeting, you can use this tab to store the connection information for your NetMeeting contacts.

11. From the Select or Add New drop-down field, select an email address to use to find the contact.

12. Enter the address of the directory server you want to use to find this person.

13. When you finish entering the contact information that you want to track, click the OK button.

EDITING A CONTACT

The following steps walk you through editing an entry in your Contact list:

1. With the Address Book open, select the entry you want to edit.

2. Click the Preferences button, or open the File menu and select Properties (Alt+Enter).

3. Click the tab that stores the information you need to edit. Most likely this is the Personal tab because you probably want to edit the email address.

4. To edit the email address, click the Edit button.

5. Place your cursor in the highlighted email field, and then edit the entry to reflect the necessary changes to the email address.

6. When you finish making your changes, click the OK button.

ADDING A GROUP

Groups are used to organize mass delivery of email messages. As you develop groups of friends on the Internet, you may find yourself sending those individuals the same email messages. To make this process easier, simply collect those names under a single nickname and then send your messages. The following steps help you with this task:

1. Open the Start menu, select Programs, and then select Windows Address Book. If you already have Outlook Express running, you can click the Address Book button, or you can open the Tools menu and select Address Book (Ctrl+Shift+B).

2. Click the New Group button, or open the File menu and select New Group (Ctrl+G).

3. Create an easily identifiable name and type it into the Group Name field (see Figure 10.4).

Figure 10.4 The Group Properties dialog box enables you to create personal groups for distributing mass mail messages.

4. Click the Select Members button. If you want to create a New Contact, you can do so by clicking the New Contact button.

5. From the Select Group members dialog box, click the names of the individuals that you want to include in your group from the left window. Hold down the Ctrl key to select multiple names.

6. Click the Select button (see Figure 10.5).

7. When all your names have been added to the Members list, click OK.

8. Click OK on the Group Properties dialog box. You see your new group listed below the main Address Book icon on the left side of your Windows Address Book screen.

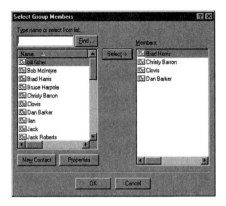

FIGURE 10.5   The Select Group Members dialog box enables you to add members to your groups.

DELETING AN ENTRY

Addresses change often, and sometimes the time comes when you no longer want to correspond with a specific individual. In this case, you may want to delete a Contact. Follow these steps:

1. With the Windows Address Book open, select the entry that you want to delete.

2. Click the Delete button on the toolbar, or open the File menu and select Delete. The entry immediately disappears from your Contact list and from all your groups.

IMPORTING ADDRESSES

As you continue using Internet email, you may find that you have switched from one email client to another or that you have a business associate or friend who wants to share his or her address book with you.

1. Open the Start menu, select Programs, and then select Windows Address Book. If you already have Outlook Express running, you can click the Address Book button, or you can open the Tools menu and select Address Book (Ctrl+Shift+B).

2. Open the File menu, select Import, and then select Address Book.

3. Select the type of Address Book you want to import into your existing address book. The options are shown in Figure 10.6.

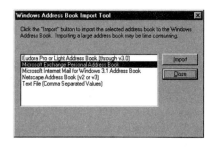

Figure 10.6   The Windows Address Book Import Tool provides you with a means of importing information directly into your existing address book.

4. After you have selected the appropriate import type, you need to follow the instructions laid out for you in the wizard that runs. For the Netscape, Eudora, and Internet Mail imports, you are simply asked for the directory in which the address book is stored. If you are importing a Windows Explorer address book, you are asked to select the specific profile from which you want to import addresses and then the specific address book to use.

In this lesson, you learned how to create and edit address book entries, create personal mailing lists, import address books from other programs, and use the variety of LDAP directories on the Internet to increase the size of your personal Address book. In the next lesson, you learn about the various methods you can use to organize your email.

EMAIL MAINTENANCE

In this lesson, you learn how to manage your incoming email.

SORTING YOUR EMAIL

One of the most frustrating things about email is the lack of organization. All your messages automatically come into one folder and stay there until you have the time to do something about it. In Outlook Express, this problem is compounded if you have multiple email addresses from which messages are collected. Fortunately, there's an easy way for you to have this information sorted and stored.

Outlook Express includes some useful tools for separating this information. You can easily retrieve mail for all your personal and business accounts and keep it separate. Outlook Express enables you to create subfolders within the Inbox or any other folder that you want. This means you can easily filter all your incoming mail into specific areas—so personal messages can go into one folder, business-related messages can automatically be placed in another folder, and each of your mailing list messages can be sorted into a folder of its own. This can save you time, and it enables you to tackle the important messages, leaving the rest for later.

CREATING FOLDERS

The following steps walk you through creating a folder:

1. Open the File menu, select Folder, and then select New Folder. The Create Folder dialog box appears (see Figure 11.1).

FIGURE 11.1 You can create a new folder under any folder in Outlook Express, including those that are installed by default.

2. Type the name for your folder in the Folder Name field. For example, you might type Personal Inbox as the name of a subfolder in which you want to store your personal messages.

3. You can place your new folder wherever you want in your Outlook Express folder hierarchy. Simply highlight the name of the folder in which you want to create the subfolder. For example, click Inbox.

4. Click the OK button.

MOVING MESSAGES INTO FOLDERS

After you have created a series of folders, you need to organize your existing messages into them. Follow these steps to move your messages into the folders you have created:

1. Select the first message that you want to move to your new folder.

2. Right-click the entry and select Move To from the shortcut menu that appears. (Alternatively, you can open the Edit menu and select Move to Folder).

3. Select the folder that you want to place your message in, such as the Personal Inbox folder you created under the Inbox.

4. Click OK.

FILTERING MESSAGES

After you have created some folders and most of your messages are sorted into them, you need to set up Outlook Express so that it takes care of this filtering process for you. When you're using Outlook Express, you have a lot of options for controlling where specific messages go and how they get there. If you're using multiple email accounts, you can use Outlook Express's filtering system, as outlined in these steps:

1. Open the Tools menu and select Inbox Assistant.

2. Click the Add button. As you can see in Figure 11.2, you can sort messages based on the names in the To:, CC:, or From: lines, the Subject: lines of your message headers, the account through which you received the messages, or the messages' size.

3. There are a variety of ways that you can complete this information, so you can essentially sort each individual message into a separate folder. For example, if you're a member of a mailing list, you might enter the list name in the To: field (such as list@studiob.com). If you're using multiple email accounts, you can sort your information into personal and business folders in your Inbox. To do so, click the Account check box, and select your personal account entry.

4. In the Perform the Following Action section, click the Move To button.

5. Click the Folder button.

6. Select the Personal Inbox folder you created earlier.

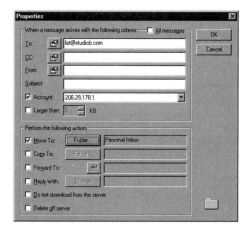

FIGURE 11.2   The properties for each Inbox Assistant filter enable you to sort information into specific filters.

7. Click the OK button.

8. Click OK again in the main Properties dialog box. You now have the first rule for your Inbox Assistant to follow (see Figure 11.3).

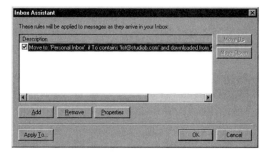

FIGURE 11.3   The Inbox Assistant shows the list of rules that have been created. Those with checked boxes are active.

9. Click OK to save the rule you created.

After you have created a rule for your Inbox Assistant to follow, anytime you download messages, they are automatically sorted into the folders that you have configured.

DELETING OLD EMAIL MESSAGES

Part of maintaining a well-organized email system is deleting the messages that you no longer need (the ones that are simply taking up important space). To delete a message, select its messages header from the list in your folder, and click the Delete button on your toolbar or press the Delete key on your keyboard.

When you delete a message, it automatically goes to your Deleted Items folder. It remains there until you empty that folder or your scheduled backup runs, whichever comes first.

COMPACTING MAIL FOLDERS

After moving and deleting messages, you will want to *compact* your mail folders. This might sound odd, but it's a necessary form of maintenance for keeping Outlook Express functioning well.

Compacting Folders   When you compact a message folder, you simply reorganize the files it contains so that they take up less space on your hard drive. This process also removes any messages that you have marked for deletion.

To compact *all* your mail folders, open the File menu, select Folders, and then select Compact All Folders. The dialog box shown in Figure 11.4 appears, showing you the progress of your folders being compacted.

FIGURE 11.4   Outlook Express names each folder as it compacts it.

If you want to compact *a single folder*, switch to the folder you want to compact, click the folder name heading, and select it from the list of available folders (see Figure 11.5). Then open the File menu, select Folder, and select Compact.

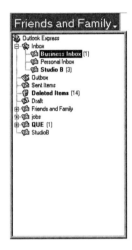

Figure 11.5 Use the folder heading to select a new folder to view.

Configuring Your Email Options

As you compact your folders and delete your messages, you may want to set up your system to automatically remove messages you delete. The following steps teach you how to configure this option:

1. Open the Tools menu and select Options.

2. Click the General tab.

3. Check the Empty Messages from the Deleted Items Folders on Exit option.

4. Click the Apply button, and then click OK.

In this lesson, you learned how to manually organize your email messages into folders and how to automatically organize them by using filters. In the next lesson, you learn how to make Outlook 97 work with Outlook Express.

USING OUTLOOK EXPRESS WITH OUTLOOK 97

In this lesson, you learn how to use Outlook 97 in conjunction with Outlook Express.

INTRODUCING OUTLOOK 97

Early in 1997, Microsoft released its Office 97 package. This software included Outlook 97, which is Microsoft's all-in-one desktop information manager. Outlook 97 includes an email Inbox, a Contact list, a scheduling Calendar, a Task List, a contact Journal, and a location to which you can track notes on your communications exchanges.

Outlook 97 is organized in a fashion very similar to Outlook Express, but it has more features. Outlook 97 provides you with a short two- or three-line start to each of your messages so that you can see what the first part of the message is and who it's from. Figure 12.1 shows the Outlook 97 window.

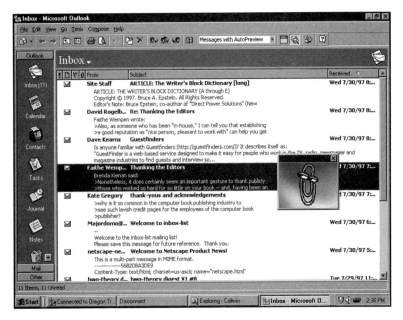

Figure 12.1 The Outlook 97 Inbox lets you look at the start of each message.

Importing Message Folders

If you use both Outlook Express and Outlook 97, you can import your mail message folders so that you don't end up with messages scattered between two different programs. Although Outlook Express makes it very easy to import information from Outlook 97, it's very hard for you to reverse the process. The following steps show you how to import your messages from Outlook 97:

1. Open the File menu, select Import, and select Messages.

2. Select Microsoft Outlook from the list of available message formats.

3. Click the Next button.

4. The location of your Outlook messages should have already been found for you. If not, click the Browse button and select the directory in which you have stored your message folders.

5. After you locate the message folders, you are asked to select the specific folders from which you want to import information (see Figure 12.2). Click the Selected Folders option button, and then select the Inbox folder.

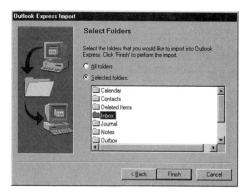

FIGURE 12.2   The Outlook Express Import function enables you to select the specific folders that you want to import into your new Internet mail client.

6. Click Finish.

IMPORTING YOUR PERSONAL ADDRESS BOOK

When you're switching from Outlook 97 to Outlook Express, you don't want to lose access to all the addresses you have stored. The easiest way to avoid this is to import all your Outlook 97 addresses into Outlook Express. Follow these steps:

1. Open the File menu, select Import, and select Address Book.

2. Select Microsoft Exchange Personal Address Book.

3. Click Import.

4. Select the Outlook 97 Profile from which you want to import the Address book, and then click OK.

5. It only takes a moment for the Address Book import function to be completed. When you receive notification that the import was successful, click the OK button.

6. Click the Close button to remove the remaining import window.

In this lesson, you learned how to share your message folders and your personal address book with Outlook 97. In the next lesson, you learn how to use Outlook Express as a newsreader.

Subscribing to Newsgroups with Outlook Express for News

In this lesson, you learn how to connect Outlook Express to your news server.

Configuring Your Server

Before you can get started using Outlook Express, you have to get the software configured to use your news server. You will be asked to provide your email account name and password, your news server name and password, and some information about your Internet service provider.

Internet Service Provider The generic term for the company that provides your Internet connection. Your service provider also provides the information you need to configure Outlook Express.

Configuring Your Server

When you run Outlook Express, you need to make sure you're connecting to the proper news server. To do this, follow these steps:

1. Open the Start menu, select Programs, Internet Explorer, and then select Outlook Express.

Running the First Time   The first time you run Outlook Express, the configuration process starts automatically.

2. Open the Tools menu and select Accounts.

3. Click the Add button and select News. This opens a screen similar to the one shown in Figure 13.1.

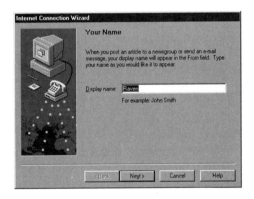

Figure 13.1   The first screen of the Internet Connection Wizard for configuring your news server.

4. Type your name in the Display Name field, and then click Next.

5. Enter your full email address in the E-Mail Address field, and then click Next.

6. Type the full address of your news server in the News (NNTP) Server field, and then click Next.

 Do I Log in to the News Server?   Although most Internet service providers don't require you to log in to the News server you use, you should check with your service provider to see if logging in is required. If you need to log in, check the My News Server Requires Me to Log In check box, and then enter your login name and password on the next screen.

7. Type a name for your news connection in the Internet News Account Name field, and then click Next.

8. You now need to indicate how you connect through your provider to your news server. There are three ways to connect to your service provider. Outlook Express Mail lets you select the method most appropriate for you. Choose from the phone line, local area network, and manual options shown in Figure 13.2. Click Next.

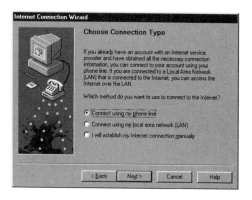

FIGURE 13.2   In the Choose Connection Type configuration screen, indicate how you connect to your service provider.

9. If you choose to use a phone connection, you need to select a Dial-Up Networking connection. If you have never connected to the Internet before, you need to create a new dial-up connection. If you have used the Internet previously, you probably already have a connection to use; in that case, select Use an Existing Dial-Up Connection, and then select a connection to use. Click Next.

If you selected either the Local Area Network or the Manual connection, you're done configuring your account. When the Congratulations screen appears, click the Finish button, and you can start using Outlook Express.

10. When you complete the configuration, click the Finish button. If you want to make changes to your settings, click the Back button until you find the option you want to adjust, make the adjustment, and use the Next button to return to the final screen.

CONFIGURING YOUR MESSAGE WINDOWS

It's simplest to read your news articles in an easy-to-read font. To configure your message window font, follow these steps:

1. Open the Tools menu and select Options.

2. Click the General tab.

3. Check the Make Outlook Express My Default News Reader check box.

4. Click the Send tab to see the options shown in Figure 13.3.

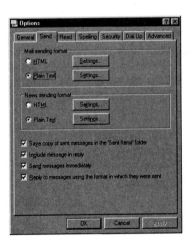

FIGURE 13.3   The Send tab of the Options dialog box allows you to control the format in which your messages are sent.

5. In the News Sending Format section of the dialog box, select either HTML or Plain Text for your news articles.

6. Click the OK button.

GETTING A LIST OF NEWSGROUPS

After you configure Outlook Express, the next step is to retrieve a list of available newsgroups. Outlook Express has no default newsgroups, so you have to find those you want and select them yourself. You can read articles in newsgroups that you haven't subscribed to.

Follow these steps to find the newsgroups and see what's available:

1. With Outlook Express running, scroll through the list of folders and select the name of your news server, as shown in Figure 13.4. (Alternatively, you can open the Go menu and select News.) This enables you to automatically connect to your Internet service provider.

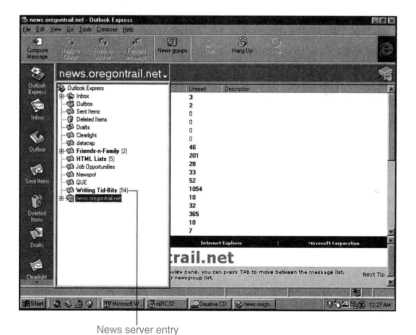

News server entry

FIGURE 13.4   The folder list showing your news server entries.

2. After you're connected, Outlook Express asks you whether you want to download the list of available newsgroups. Click **OK**, and a list of the newsgroups appears onscreen as your news server downloads it to your computer.

3. When all the newsgroups have been downloaded and sorted, Outlook Express displays the Newsgroups window, shown in Figure 13.5. It lists all the newsgroups to which you have access.

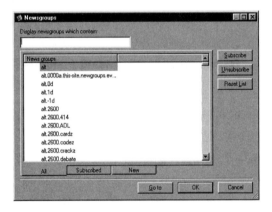

Figure 13.5   The list of newsgroups available from your service provider's news server.

This list initially shows you all the newsgroups available from your news server. However, you can sort this list so that you see only the groups in which you're interested.

Sorting the Newsgroup List

If you had to browse through a list of more than 22,000 newsgroups, it might be impossible to find newsgroups that discuss topics you're interested in. To assist in this search, Outlook Express provides a sorting utility that looks for specific words and phrases in your list of newsgroup names. Here's how to sort the list:

1. With Outlook Express running, open the Go menu and select News.

2. Open the Tools menu and select Newsgroups, or click the Newsgroups button on the toolbar. The Newsgroups dialog box opens.

3. In the Display Newsgroups Which Contain field, type a topic that's of interest to you. For example, you could type barefoot to see a list of newsgroups related to bare feet (see Figure 13.6).

Don't Press Enter You do not have to press Enter after typing a topic; as you type, the list of newsgroups is sorted automatically.

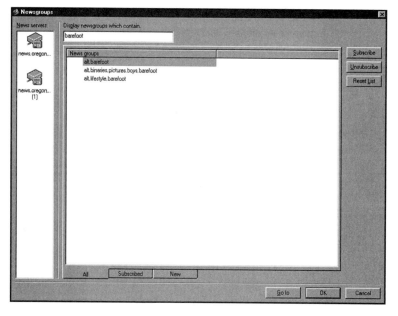

Figure 13.6 The list now displays only newsgroups discussing your specified topic.

SUBSCRIBING TO NEWSGROUPS

After you subscribe to a newsgroup, the subject information for each article in that newsgroup is automatically downloaded every time you connect to your news server. You don't need to subscribe to a newsgroup in order to review its messages; however, subscribing does make it easier to find the newsgroup again later.

 Subscribe   The process used to mark a list of favorite newsgroups that you read frequently. This lets you access your favorite newsgroups in a manner similar to that in which you access your favorite web sites.

Follow these steps to subscribe to a newsgroup:

1. With Outlook Express running, select your news server from the folders drop-down list or the Outlook toolbar. (Or, open the Go menu and select News.)

2. Because you already have a list of newsgroups, open the Tools menu and select Newsgroups.

3. Read through the list of newsgroup names until you find one that interests you. Click to select the one you want.

 TIP   **Reading Unsubscribed Newsgroups**   To read the messages in a newsgroup you have not subscribed to, click the Go To button at the bottom of your Newsgroups dialog box.

4. With a group name selected, click Subscribe. You can repeat this process for as many newsgroups as you're interested in. In the newsgroup list, a newspaper icon appears to the left of each newsgroup to which you've subscribed.

5. To see the list of newsgroups you've subscribed to, click the Subscribed tab.

In this lesson, you learned how to configure Outlook Express to contact your News server and subscribe to the newsgroups you're interested in. In the next lesson, you will learn how to work with the articles in your subscribed newsgroups.

14

LESSON

WORKING WITH NEWSGROUP ARTICLES

In this lesson, you learn how to download specific articles so that you can read them at your leisure.

DOWNLOADING ARTICLE HEADERS

Outlook Express enables you to control how much of your time and hard drive space is going to be taken up by the articles you download from newsgroups. The first time you connect to a newsgroup, you have to download the *message headers*. The headers are the only part of the messages that are downloaded automatically.

Message Header   The portion of the message containing information about the original author of the message, whom the article was sent to, and the subject of the message.

The following steps show you how to download the new message headers for your subscribed newsgroups:

1. With Outlook Express running, scroll through the folders list and select the newsgroup you want to read. (Alternatively, you can open the Go menu, select News, and choose a newsgroup from the screen shown in Figure 14.1.)

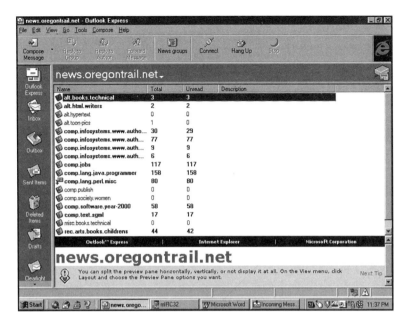

FIGURE 14.1 The main Outlook Express window, showing your available newsgroups.

2. Double-click the newsgroup you're interested in. Outlook Express automatically connects to your service provider, connects to your news server, and downloads the headers for that newsgroup.

Printing Messages You can print a message only from the message window (see the section "Printing Articles" later in this lesson). However, you can reply to the original author, reply to the newsgroup, or forward to another individual or group from the preview window.

TIP   **Downloading Headers**   Outlook Express does not have to automatically download each message when you select it. Instead, you want it to download all selected messages at one time to reduce your connect time (which leaves your phone line open for incoming calls and also keeps your Internet connection charges to a minimum). You can select all the messages you want to read while you're offline, connect for a few minutes to download them from the server, and then disconnect before reading them.

TAGGING ARTICLES

As you read through the message headers, you can find out what type of conversations are taking place and decide whether you want to participate in them. The bodies of messages take up large amounts of space on your hard drive. And if files are attached to the messages, they take up even more space. By taking advantage of the option of reading the message headers before downloading the entire message, you can conserve your online time and your hard drive space—two major considerations when using a computer on the Internet. When you find particular articles that you would like to read in their entirety, you *tag* them. To tag an article, perform the following steps:

1. Open Outlook Express but don't connect to the Internet.

2. Open your newsgroups list and select a newsgroup to read—one that you have already downloaded the headers for.

3. Select a message that you didn't view while online. The preview window tells you that the message is not cached and needs to be downloaded.

4. To tag this article, right-click the article's header and select Mark Message for Download from the shortcut menu. Outlook Express displays a green arrow icon to the left of

the article (see Figure 14.2). This icon identifies articles that will be downloaded the next time you connect to your service provider.

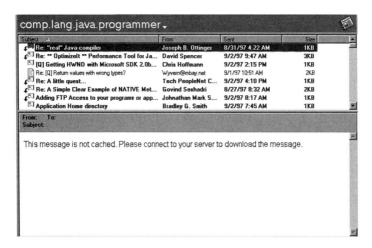

FIGURE 14.2 Messages with a green arrow have been tagged for downloading.

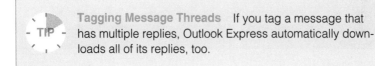

Tagging Message Threads If you tag a message that has multiple replies, Outlook Express automatically downloads all of its replies, too.

DOWNLOADING SELECTED MESSAGES

In the previous sections, you tagged some messages you wanted to read. Now you need to get those messages from the news server to your computer. To download all tagged messages, follow these steps:

1. Click the Connect button to connect to your service provider.

2. Open the Tools menu and select Download All. This starts the automatic retrieval process for all the articles that you have marked. The Post and Download window, shown in Figure 14.3, shows you the progress of your download.

3. When the articles are completely downloaded, double-click one to see the entire message.

FIGURE 14.3   You can monitor the progress as Outlook Express downloads your articles.

OPENING ARTICLES

Generally, you download messages so that you can read them. Outlook Express provides you with a preview window so that you can skim a message quickly, without waiting for a message to open all the way. You can use the preview window to read your messages and to perform any other message-specific action.

When you need to open an article in a true article window, double-click the message header. This opens the message in its own window (see Figure 14.4). If a message is a reply, greater than marks (>>) appear in front of the original message's text. As you can see, this message is a reply to a previously posted message that was also a reply.

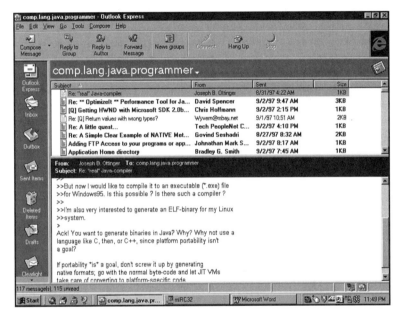

Figure 14.4 The article window showing a message sent to the newsgroup.

Printing Articles

You might read a message and decide you want to print it (to keep on file or to pass along to a friend, for example). Printing an article is quite easy; just follow these steps:

1. Double-click a message's header to open the message in the message window.

2. Open the File menu and select Print (Ctrl+P).

3. In the Print dialog box, select the printer, number of copies, and print range. Click OK.

Quick Print   With a message open, you can simply click the Print toolbar button to have the article sent to the currently selected printer.

THREADING ARTICLES

A *thread* is made up of the original message and all responses to that message chained together to create a flowing conversation. By following a message thread, you can read the original message and everyone's responses to it. Then you can read the responses to the responses until you have read the entire conversation.

In the Outlook Express window, a plus sign next to a message indicates that the message has a thread of responses. You click the plus sign to see the headers of all messages sent as responses to that original message. If any of those responses has generated responses, a plus sign appears next to the first response to show that the thread continues. Again, you click the plus sign to see the next level of responses. A minus sign appears next to a message when you have displayed all of its responses.

To follow a thread of articles, take these steps:

1. With Outlook Express open, scroll through the messages you downloaded. Search for one that has a plus sign in front of it. Click that symbol.

2. Scroll through the thread list to see all the responses to the original message (see Figure 14.5). If you see more plus signs, you can click them to expand the thread further.

The plus sign [+] notes that the message
is part of an expandable thread.

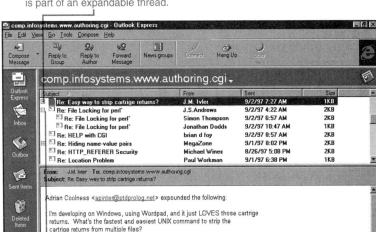

The minus sign [-] shows that a message's
thread has been completely expanded.

FIGURE 14.5 Plus and minus signs identify a thread: original
messages and their responses.

REPLYING TO A NEWSGROUP

When you want to respond to a news article with a public state-
ment, you respond to the entire group. This enables everyone,
including the casual observer, to read your message. Posting messages to an entire newsgroup is often the best way to get an answer to your question. To respond to an entire newsgroup,
perform the following steps:

1. With Outlook Express open, select a message that you
   have read and would like to comment on. Click the Reply

to Group button. The original message opens in the message window (see Figure 14.6).

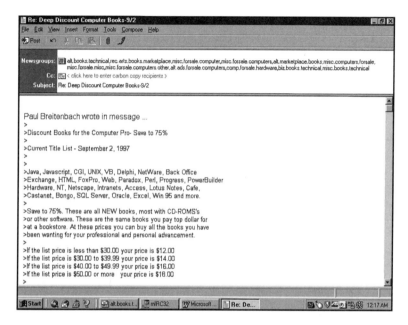

FIGURE 14.6   A response addressed to an entire newsgroup.

2. As you can see, the Newsgroups field automatically displays the original newsgroup's name. The Subject field contains the subject of the original message with the reply tag (Re:) added, and the cursor appears in the body of the message where you will enter your comments. Add all the comments you want.

3. When you finish your message, click the Send button. Outlook Express places a copy of your message in the Outbox to be posted to the newsgroup the next time you connect to your service provider.

REPLYING TO THE ORIGINAL AUTHOR

Sometimes you read something that you want to talk to the author—and only the author—about. Maybe you want to clarify a point, or maybe you simply want to get to know that person better because you seem to have a shared interest. No matter the reason, replying to an individual is essentially the same as replying to a group, except that you use the Internet Mail client to send the information. Follow these steps:

1. With Outlook Express open, select a message that you would like to comment on. Click the Reply to Author button. The original message opens in a mail window, as shown in Figure 14.7.

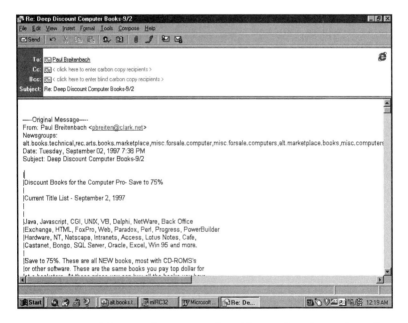

FIGURE 14.7 The email message is addressed to the author of the newsgroup article to which you are responding.

2. The To field automatically displays the original newsgroup name. The Subject field contains the subject

of the original message with the reply tag (Re:) added, and your cursor appears in the body of the message where you will enter your comments. Add any comments you want.

 Legal Email   Because you're legally responsible for email messages in the same way you're responsible for written messages, you need to make sure that your response isn't slanderous and that it contains no copyrighted information.

3. When you finish your reply, click the Send button. Outlook Express places a copy of your message in the Outbox of the Internet Mail client. The next time you connect to your service provider, the message is mailed to the selected recipients.

In this lesson, you learned to tag articles for later retrieval, download all or part of a news article, navigate through message threads, read articles, and send replies. In the next lesson, you learn how to use the Internet securely.

Using the Internet Securely

*In this lesson, you learn how to set
your security zones, manage security certificates,
and use Microsoft Wallet.*

Setting Your Security Level

Because the Internet is an interconnected series of networked
computers, any information you send can pass through many
computers before it reaches your intended destination. This fact
gives rise to a number of security concerns—not because there
have been a rash of "Information Superhighway Robberies," but
because the possibility exists that your data (business records,
proprietary trade information, or credit card numbers) might be
accessed by unauthorized individuals. Internet Explorer 4.0 has a
wide range of industry-standard security measures in place. For
example, most web sites involving credit card transactions are run
on computers known as secure servers. When Internet Explorer
encounters a secure server, a small lock appears in the status bar.

Microsoft has devised a system of security zones because you
don't do all your computing with one type of web site. Some
types of network connections can be trusted more than others.
Your company intranet, for example, is far more of a known en-
tity than unsolicited email advertisements offering a download
too good to be true. You can set different security levels (High,
Medium, Low, and Custom) for each zone.

Internet Explorer has four different security zones:

- **Local Intranet**   Defined by your system administrator, this zone incorporates your in-house network connections. The default security level for this zone is Medium.

- **Trusted Sites**   This zone includes sites that you believe to be trustworthy and are confident enough to download or run files from. You assign the sites to this security zone where the default security level is Low.

- **Restricted Sites**   Sites that you deem to be untrustworthy and that you want to prevent from downloading files to your system are grouped in this zone. You assign sites to this security zone where the default security level is High.

- **Internet Zone**   Every site not included in the other security zones. The default security level for this zone is Medium.

To alter the security level settings for any of the zones, follow these steps:

1. From the View menu, select Internet Options.

2. From the Options dialog box, click the Security tab.

3. From the Security tab, as shown in Figure 15.1, select the security zone you want to change from the Zone drop-down list.

4. From the security level area, select one of the following:

   - **High**   Doesn't download certain programs and alerts you to the attempt.

   - **Medium**   Warns of any file attempting to load onto your system.

   - **Low**   Neither warns about, nor avoids, any file download.

   - **Custom**   Enables advanced users and developers to select specific settings for active content and other potential security risks.

5. After you have clicked the option button next to your selection, click OK.

6. Click OK again to close the Options dialog box.

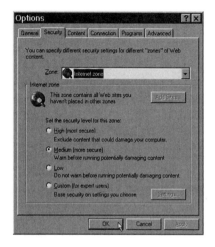

FIGURE 15.1   The Security tab manages web security.

ASSIGNING WEB SITES TO A SECURITY ZONE

Two of the security zones depend on you to add web sites to their lists. Both Trusted Sites and Restricted Sites are completely user-defined. To assign a web site to a security zone, follow these steps:

1. From the View menu, select Options.

2. From the Options dialog box, click the Security tab.

3. Select either Trusted Sites or Restricted Sites in the Zone box by clicking the option arrow.

   The Add Sites button becomes active.

4. Click the Add Sites button.

5. From the Trusted Sites Zone (or Restricted Sites Zone) dialog box, as shown in Figure 15.2, type the URL for the web site you would like to assign in the Add this Web Site to the Zone box. You must use the complete URL—for instance, **http://www.microsoft.com**.

6. After you have typed in the complete URL, click the Add button.

   The URL appears in the Web Sites box.

7. To clear a URL from the list, select it and click the Remove button.

8. Click the OK button when you have finished assigning your web sites.

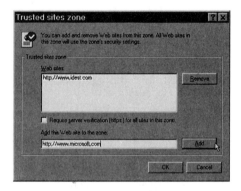

FIGURE 15.2   You can assign web sites to either the Trusted or Restricted Sites security zones.

UNDERSTANDING SECURITY CERTIFICATES

When you buy software in a store, it's labeled and shrink-wrapped—you can be fairly certain who the publisher is and that the software has not be tampered with. There are no such guarantees, however, when downloading software over the Internet.

Internet Explorer recognizes a set of industry-standard security certificates to assure that the software publisher and the software are "as advertised." Whenever you download software from a secure web server, Internet Explorer first downloads a security certificate. When the software begins to download, Internet Explorer checks it against the security certificate to make sure that the software is from the correct publisher and is intact.

If the software appears to have been tampered with, Internet Explorer issues a warning. If the software has not been digitally signed (so it can't be verified), Internet Explorer asks if you would like to continue the download of unverified software.

You can view and delete the security certificates installed on your system during transactions. Follow these steps to manage your security certificates:

1. From the View menu, select Folder Options

2. From the Options dialog box, click the Content tab.

3. In the Certificates section, click one of the optional buttons:

   - **Personal**   Lists certificates that identify you to secure servers.

   - **Authorities**   Lists certificates from secure servers you have visited.

   - **Publishers**   Lists certificates from publishers that you have accepted. This permits any software from these publishers to be loaded on your system without asking permission.

   Clicking any of the three Certificate buttons opens its respective list.

4. From the Personal or Authorities dialog box, select any certificate listed to enable the View Certificate and Delete buttons.

5. To see details of the certificate, click the View Certificate button.

6. To remove the certificate from your system, click Delete.

7. Click OK to close the Personal, Sites, or Publisher Certificate dialog box.

8. Click OK to close the Options dialog box.

 Certificate Accidentally Removed If you unintentionally remove a security certificate, you can get it back. The next time you visit a site that requires a particular certificate, the system asks if you would accept the Tcertificate.

USING MICROSOFT WALLET

As electronic credit card transactions increase, you'll find yourself typing the same 14 numbers (and an expiration date) over and over again. Internet Explorer includes a new feature that enables you to hand over a "virtual" credit card for easy-to-use, but safe, electronic transactions. Microsoft Wallet holds any amount of personal and credit card information necessary to do business over the Internet.To access Microsoft Wallet, follow these steps:

1. From the View menu, select Internet Options.

2. From the Options dialog box, click the Programs tab.

3. From the Programs tab, select one of the two buttons in the Personal Information section:

   • **Address Manager** Enables you to set up your address information so it will not have to be retyped for every site.

   • **Payment Manager** Enables you to input credit card information so it will not have to be retyped for every site.

4. If you want to change your address information, click the Address Manager button. To add new information, click

the Add button and fill out the form. Click the Close button when you are finished.

5. If you want to change your credit card information, click the Payment Manager button.

6. Click the Add button shown in Figure 15.3, and choose one of the available credit card types.

7. The Credit Card Wizard opens. Click Next.

8. Fill out the required information. Click Next.

9. Enter a password in the first box. Retype the password in the second box. Click Finish.

10. Click Close to close the Address or Payment Manager dialog box.

11. Click OK to close the Options dialog box.

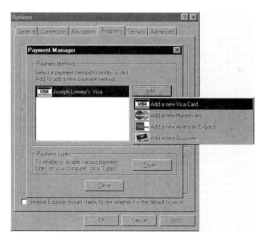

FIGURE 15.3   Adding a new credit card to the Microsoft Wallet.

In this lesson, you learned how to set your security level, how to manage security certificates, and how to use Microsoft Wallet. In the next lesson, you learn how to take advantage of Internet Explorer's new integrated desktop.

16 LESSON

INTEGRATING THE WEB AND THE PC

In this lesson, you learn how to install the Web Integrated Desktop and learn what it brings to your computer.

The biggest news in Internet Explorer 4.0 is the integration of the web and your PC desktop. In the new Web Integrated Desktop, your desktop looks and works like a web page. All your folder names are underlined like links in a web page, and they open with a single-click instead of a double-click. You can display web content directly on your desktop, customize folder windows to look and work like web pages, and use the same toolbars and menu bars in both folder and browser windows. For a total immersion experience on the web, you can use Full Screen view in the browser window so that everything but the web page itself is hidden.

With the Web Integrated Desktop installed, you can browse the web from anywhere on your computer: the Start menu, your Favorites menu, toolbars, the taskbar, and icons on your desktop. A single-click launches your browser and heads for the web site. You use the same window and navigation tools to browse your hard drive, the company network, and the Internet.

Shell Integration Shell Integration is computerese for the theory behind the installed feature of the Web Integrated Desktop; it refers to the integration of your computer desktop and the Internet into one seamless and cohesive unit, or *shell*, that looks and acts like a web page.

INSTALLING THE WEB INTEGRATED DESKTOP

The Web Integrated Desktop brings the Internet to your computer. You may have already installed the Web Integrated Desktop when you installed Internet Explorer 4.0; if not, follow these steps to install the Web Integrated Desktop:

1. Click the Start button.

2. Point to Settings, and then click Control Panel.

3. Double-click Add/Remove Programs.

4. Click Microsoft Internet Explorer 4.0, and then click Add/Remove.

5. Click the Add Windows Desktop Update from Web site option button, and then click OK. If you don't see the option, then the Web Integrated Desktop is already installed, and you can click the Cancel button in each dialog box to back out of the installation process.

6. Internet Explorer 4.0 goes online to retrieve the files it needs, and then installs them. Follow the steps in the online wizard.

TIP   **Is It Installed Already?**   If the icon titles on your desktop are underlined, then the Web Integrated Desktop is already installed. If they're not underlined, the Web Integrated Desktop may be installed, but with some settings changed. In that case, follow the preceding steps to find out for sure. To learn how to change the icon title settings, look at Lesson 17, "The Active Desktop and Your PC."

If you want to remove the Web Integrated Desktop and use Internet Explorer 4.0 as a simple browser, follow these steps:

1. Click the Start button.
2. Point to Settings, and then click Control Panel.
3. Double-click Add/Remove Programs.
4. Click Microsoft Internet Explorer 4.0, and then click Add/Remove.
5. Click the Remove Web Integrated Desktop, but Keep the Internet Explorer 4.0 Browser option button.
6. Click OK.

You can install the Web Integrated Desktop again later if you leave the Internet Explorer 4.0 setup files on your hard drive.

Elements of the Web Integrated Desktop

The Web Integrated Desktop contains many new elements designed to make it easier to integrate the Internet into your desktop. Among the new elements are a common Standard toolbar at the top of every folder and browser window, a taskbar with expanded features, a pumped-up new Start menu, Explorer bars for every folder and browser window, and the new Active Desktop, which puts live web content on your computer screen.

The Common Standard Toolbar

The new Standard toolbar provides you with consistent navigation methods, whether you're browsing your computer's hard drive, the company intranet, or the Internet. The new Standard toolbar is called a *smart* toolbar because it changes to give you just the buttons you need for the type of information you're looking at. As you can see in Figure 16.1, if you're looking at a folder on your hard drive, the toolbar has buttons to cut, copy, and paste files and folders; however, if you're looking at a web page (see Figure 16.2), the toolbar replaces those buttons with Stop, Refresh, and Home buttons.

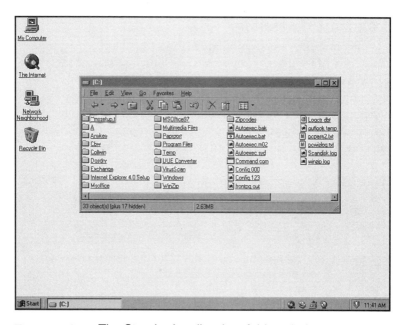

FIGURE 16.1   The Standard toolbar in a folder window.

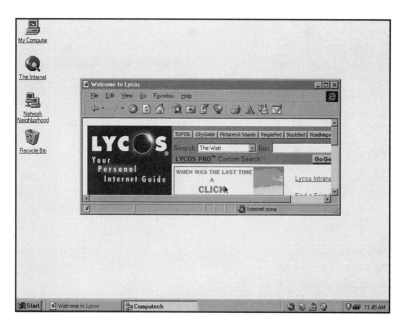

FIGURE 16.2   The Standard toolbar in a browser window.

THE NEW TASKBAR

The new taskbar is much more useful than the old taskbar. It has its own set of toolbars, all of which are shown in Figure 16.3. The toolbars can be resized, rearranged, and dragged away from the taskbar to float on the desktop. Another new feature is the toggle capability for open windows. As before, each open window has a button on the taskbar, but now you can minimize a window and then open it again just by clicking its button on the taskbar.

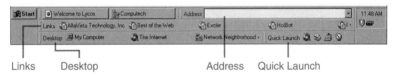

Links   Desktop   Address   Quick Launch

FIGURE 16.3   The new taskbar, with all of its toolbars displayed.

THE NEW START MENU

The new Start menu works just like the old Start menu, but now it does more. It has your list of Favorites, so you can launch your browser and go to a favorite web site directly from the Start menu. In addition, you can customize the Start menu. You can rearrange your list of Favorites or Programs by dragging an icon to a new location on the list (which means you don't have to keep them in alphabetical order), and you can add a shortcut to a folder by dragging it onto the Start button.

THE EXPLORER BARS

The Explorer bars are specialized toolbars that sit vertically on the left side of the browser window. Figure 16.4 shows one of the four Explorer bars; the other three Explorer bars are the Search bar, the Favorites bar, and the Channels bar.

To learn more about the Explorer bars, see Chapter 3, "Searching the World Wide Web."

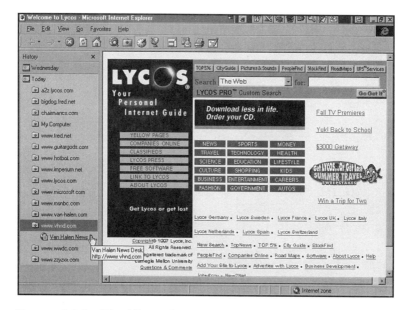

FIGURE 16.4   The History bar is an Explorer bar that keeps a history of web sites you've visited.

THE ACTIVE DESKTOP

The Active Desktop is the part of the Web Integrated Desktop that brings live web content, such as a stock-market ticker display like the one shown in Figure 16.5, to your computer. It also enables you to customize your desktop so that it behaves like a web page, with single-click access to folders and files and desktop shortcuts to web sites.

Web pages that are regularly updated with current information, called Desktop Components, can reside on your Active Desktop where they're instantly available. You have an Internet full of choices for your desktop background. To learn more about the Active Desktop, see Lesson 17, "The Active Desktop and Your PC."

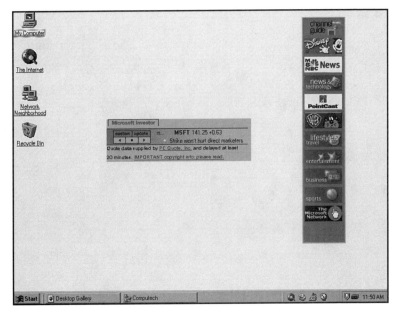

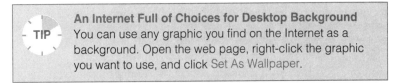

Figure 16.5 This stock ticker and Channel Guide are desktop components that reside on your Active Desktop.

An Internet Full of Choices for Desktop Background
TIP You can use any graphic you find on the Internet as a background. Open the web page, right-click the graphic you want to use, and click Set As Wallpaper.

In this lesson, you learned about installing the Web Integrated Desktop and what you'll find on your new desktop. In the next lesson, you learn about Internet Explorer 4.0's new Active Desktop.

THE ACTIVE DESKTOP AND YOUR PC

*In this lesson, you learn how to use
and customize Internet Explorer 4.0's Active Desktop.*

ABOUT THE ACTIVE DESKTOP

The Active Desktop is a combination of your normal desktop (the icon layer) and a layer of active web content that lays on top (the HTML layer). You can turn the Active Desktop on or off, which adds or removes the layer of active web content.

To turn the Active Desktop off (or back on again), follow these steps:

1. Right-click an empty spot on the desktop background.

2. Point to Active Desktop, and click View As Web Page. If the View as Web Page command has a check mark next to it, the Active Desktop is turned on.

Under everything on the Active Desktop is the background, which can be wallpapered with a picture, an HTML page on your hard drive, or a graphic that you pick up from the web.

To use an HTML page on your hard drive as a background, follow these steps:

1. Right-click an empty spot on the desktop, and click Properties.

2. On the Background tab, click Browse.

3. In the Browse dialog box, select HTML Document in the Files of Type box.

4. Browse through your hard drive to an HTML page you want, select the file name, and then click Open. The HTML page appears in the preview window in the Display Properties dialog box.

5. In the Display box, select Center, Tile, or Stretch. Center places the wallpaper, with its original dimensions, in the center of the desktop; Tile pastes copies of the wallpaper all over the desktop, like a mosaic; and Stretch resizes the wallpaper so that a single image covers the entire desktop.

6. Click OK.

 Is It On? The Active Desktop must be turned on to use an HTML page as desktop wallpaper.

To use a picture on your hard drive as a background (like the one shown in Figure 17.1), follow these steps:

1. Right-click an empty spot on the desktop, and click Properties.

2. On the Background tab, click Browse.

3. In the Browse dialog box, select Picture in the Files of Type box.

4. Browse through your hard drive to the graphic file you want, select the file name, and then click Open. The picture appears in the preview window in the Display Properties dialog box.

5. In the Display box, select Center, Tile, or Stretch, and then click OK.

FIGURE 17.1   A scanned photo set as a background.

To use a graphic you find on the Internet as a background (like the one shown in Figure 17.2), follow these steps:

1. Launch your browser and find a graphic you like on the Internet (perhaps a company logo, or a photograph of your favorite celebrity).

2. Right-click the graphic and click Set As Wallpaper. The graphic appears on your desktop, centered. If that's what you want, you're done; if you want to tile or stretch the graphic, continue to step 3.

3. Right-click an empty spot on the desktop, and click Properties.

4. On the Background tab, in the Display box, select Center, Tile, or Stretch, and then click OK.

FIGURE 17.2   This background is a centered web site graphic.

THE ICON LAYER

The icon layer is your normal desktop, with your icons, taskbar, and wallpaper. If you turn off the Active Desktop, what remains is the icon layer.

THE HTML LAYER

The HTML layer is a transparent layer on top of the icon layer. It holds Desktop components like the Channel Guide, web pages you subscribe to and get updated regularly, and other items like a stock-market ticker or weather map that you can download from Microsoft. (See Lesson 18, "Using Desktop Components," to learn more about adding live items to the HTML layer.)

USING SHORTCUT ICONS ON THE DESKTOP

Whether the Active Desktop is turned on or off, you can add shortcut icons to your desktop so that you can get to work more quickly. You can place shortcut icons on your desktop to launch a program, or to open a specific file, and you can arrange the icons to be as neat or as messy as you want. You can create shortcut icons to anything: programs, files, folder windows, and web pages.

LAUNCHING PROGRAMS AND OPENING FILES

How easy is it to launch programs and open files with shortcut icons? All you have to do is click the icon. You've probably already done it, by opening the My Computer window (even though the My Computer icon isn't a shortcut, it works exactly the same way).

If your desktop is in Internet Explorer 4.0's single-click mode, one click launches the program or file. If your desktop is in the classic Windows 95 double-click mode, one click selects the icon, and a double-click launches the file or program.

ADDING ICONS TO THE DESKTOP

Adding shortcut icons to your desktop is almost as fast as using them. To add a shortcut icon for a file or folder, follow these steps:

1. Open the My Computer window and browse to find the folder or file you want.

2. Press and hold the right mouse button and drag the file or folder you want from the window onto the desktop.

3. On the shortcut menu that appears, click Create Shortcut(s) Here.

To add a shortcut icon for a program, follow these steps:

1. Open the My Computer window and browse to find the program file you want. It will probably be in a program folder and have the program-specific icon next to it, and the file name will end in .exe.

2. Press and hold the right mouse button and drag the file from the window onto the desktop.

3. On the shortcut menu that appears, click Create Shortcut(s) Here.

To add a shortcut icon for a web link, first browse to the site. Then resize the browser window so that it's not maximized (you want to be able to drag from the browser window to your desktop). To create a shortcut to the page you're looking at, drag the icon from the Address toolbar in the browser window onto your desktop. To create a shortcut to a link on the page you're looking at, drag the link from the page onto your desktop.

Now that you've added several shortcut icons to your desktop, it might be getting a bit disorderly. You have a few options for arranging icons on your desktop:

- Right-click an empty spot on your desktop, point to Arrange Icons, and click AutoArrange. All your icons line up in columns on the left side of your desktop. If you move an icon, it will be sucked back into line.

- If AutoArrange seems too orderly, turn it off: Right-click an empty spot on your desktop, point to Arrange Icons, and click AutoArrange to remove the check mark.

- Right-click an empty spot on your desktop, and then click Line Up Icons. Your icons are aligned in a grid formation on your desktop. Each one is near where you left it, but in an orderly manner with no overlapping.

REMOVING ICONS FROM THE DESKTOP

Some of the icons on your desktop, such as My Computer or Recycle Bin, aren't shortcuts—they're the actual folder or file (and any file or folder that you save in your Desktop folder has an icon on the desktop).

 Where's my folder?   If you move or delete these icons, you move or delete the actual folder or file.

Shortcut icons have a little curving arrow in the lower-left corner. You can move or delete shortcut icons as much as you want to because they're only shortcuts and you won't be moving or deleting the actual file. To delete a shortcut icon, drag it onto the Recycle Bin.

SINGLE-CLICK MODE VERSUS DOUBLE-CLICK MODE

The Active Desktop makes your desktop work like a web page, which includes turning your desktop icons into underlined, single-click links. One drawback to the new single-click mode is that you can no longer rename an icon by clicking its title and typing a new name. If you miss that feature, you can change your Active Desktop settings back to pre-Internet Explorer 4.0 behavior.

To switch back to double-click mode, follow these steps:

1. In a browser or folder window, select View, Options.

2. On the General tab, click the Classic Style option button. This option changes your settings to the default Windows 95 settings: double-click mode and multiple windows.

3. Click OK.

You have options other than the new Web view and the Classic style. To mix and match the settings you want, follow these steps:

1. In a browser or folder window, click View, Options.

2. On the General tab, click the Custom, Based on Settings You Choose option button, and then click the Settings button.

3. On the Custom Settings dialog box (see Figure 17.3), click option buttons for the settings you want.

4. Click OK, and then click OK again.

Figure 17.3   Customize your window behavior in the Custom Settings dialog box.

In this lesson, you learned how to use and customize the Active Desktop. In the next lesson, you learn about Desktop Components, items that reside in the HTML layer of your Active Desktop.

USING DESKTOP COMPONENTS

In this lesson, you learn about
Desktop Components and how to get them onto your desktop, schedule
them, update them, and customize them.

VIEWING DESKTOP COMPONENTS

Desktop Components are ActiveX and Java objects that bring live web content to your Active Desktop. Currently they include items like a stock-market investment ticker, a national weather map, a 3-D clock, and your Channel Guide (see Figure 18.1). As time goes by, more Desktop Components will become available.

Desktop Components reside in the HTML layer of your Active Desktop. You can view them and hide them by turning your Active Desktop on or off.

 TIP **Channel Guide** When you first install Internet Explorer 4.0, the only Desktop Component you'll have is the Channel Guide.

To turn on your Active Desktop (and see your Desktop Components), follow these steps:

1. Right-click an empty spot on your desktop, and then point to Active Desktop.

2. Click View As Web Page. If the Active Desktop is turned on, the View as Web Page command has a check mark next to it.

3-D clock   Channel guide

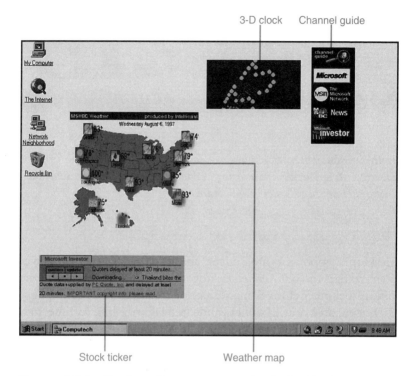

Stock ticker   Weather map

Figure 18.1 Desktop Components on the Active Desktop.

To turn the Active Desktop off (and hide all your Desktop Components), repeat the preceding steps.

Adding a Desktop Component

How do you get one of these Desktop Components onto your Active Desktop? Follow these steps:

1. Right-click an empty spot on your desktop, and then point to Active Desktop.

2. Click Customize My Desktop.

3. On the Web tab (see Figure 18.2), click the New button.

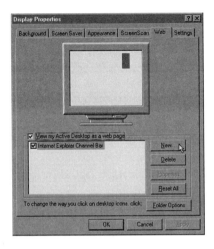

FIGURE 18.2   Find and add Desktop Components on the Web tab.

4. The New Active Desktop Item message box asks if you'd like to visit Microsoft's Active Desktop gallery. Click Yes. (If you want to add a Desktop Component from someplace other than Microsoft's Gallery, click No, and then type the path to the new item, or browse to locate it, in the New Active Desktop Item dialog box.)

5. Your browser goes online to the Microsoft Active Desktop gallery. Click an item you want to add to your desktop.

6. Your browser opens a web page that describes the item you clicked. To add the item to your desktop, click the Add to My Desktop button. A Security Alert message box asks you to confirm that you want to add a Desktop item. Click Yes.

7. In the Create a New Desktop Item dialog box that appears, you can customize the update schedule for the new Desktop Component by clicking the Customize Subscription button, or you can accept the default schedule and click OK. Your new Desktop Component is downloaded.

Changing the Default   The default update schedule is - **TIP** - AutoSchedule, which means an automatic daily update between midnight and 5:00 am if you're on a network, or whenever you go online if you use the modem in your computer. You can change the update schedule at any time; see the later section "Updating Desktop Components."

8. Your browser returns to the item's web page. From here you can add more desktop components, or return to your desktop and look at the new item.

 Where's My New Item?   If your new item doesn't appear - **TIP** - on your desktop, right-click the desktop and click Refresh.

 The Desktop Component Gallery   The Desktop Component Gallery is a collection of ActiveX and Java objects that Microsoft has assembled for you to freely download. By the time you read this, there will probably be several more items than you see pictured here. The best way to see what's available is to follow the preceding steps to add a new item and then read the Microsoft Active Gallery web page to find out what's there.

You aren't limited to the items in Microsoft's Desktop Component Gallery; any ActiveX or Java object with live web content can be displayed on your Active Desktop.

Customizing a Desktop Component

After you get a new Desktop Component onto your Active Desktop, you can resize it and move it for more convenient viewing, and for some components you can select which information is downloaded (for example, you may want to download quotes for specific stocks in the stock ticker or download weather information for a different country).

To resize a Desktop Component, follow these steps:

1. Point to an edge of the item; a border appears, and the pointer becomes a two-headed arrow.

2. Drag the border of the item to the size you want.

To move a Desktop Component, follow these steps:

1. Point to the top edge of the item. A title bar appears (see Figure 18.3).

2. Drag the title bar to relocate the item.

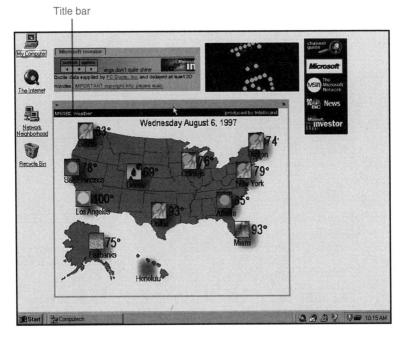

FIGURE 18.3   To move a Desktop Component, drag its title bar.

Selecting what information to download is a little different for each Desktop Component, so you need to experiment a bit with different components. In general, to customize the information that's downloaded, follow these steps:

1. Right-click the component.

2. Click Custom. If there isn't a Custom command, try clicking the item itself (for example, in the Weather Map this takes you online for weather all over the world).

3. Fill out the Properties dialog box that appears. (The dialog box is different for each item; Figure 18.4 shows the Properties dialog box for the Microsoft Investor Stock Ticker.)

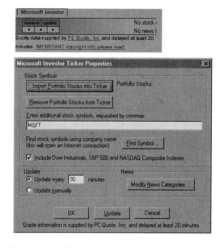

FIGURE 18.4   Select the information you want to download in the item's Properties dialog box.

UPDATING DESKTOP COMPONENTS

The magic of Desktop Components is that they're updated with current information on a regular basis. How often they are updated is up to you. You can set a regular, automatic schedule for updating, or you can update only when you decide to update. Each item has its own update schedule, so you have great flexibility.

Keep in mind that updating often means your computer will be going online often to download updated information, which can be disruptive to your normal work.

To set an update schedule, follow these steps:

1. Right-click an empty spot on the desktop.

2. Point to Active Desktop, and then click Customize My Desktop.

3. On the Web tab, select the item you want to schedule, and then click Properties.

4. On the Schedule tab, select a scheduling option.

   The AutoSchedule option works only for computers on a corporate-type network that connect to the Internet through a network server, and the item is updated whenever the item's publisher decides to update.

   If you're not on a network and you connect directly from your modem, you can select the Custom Schedule option or the Update Now option. The Custom Schedule option enables you to set a regular schedule for your modem to go online and download new information; the Update Now option enables you to update information only when you decide to update.

5. Click OK.

If you scheduled automatic updates, there's nothing else you have to do (except leave your computer on during the time when the update is scheduled so that your modem can go online and download the information).

If you set an Update Now schedule, you get updated information when you decide to update. To update your desktop items, follow these steps:

1. Right-click an empty spot on the desktop.

2. Point to Active Desktop, and then click Update Now.

HIDING A DESKTOP COMPONENT

You may not want to see all your items all the time. You can hide them, which keeps them available for viewing, but only when you want them.

To hide a Desktop Component, follow these steps:

1. Point to the top edge of the item, until the title bar appears.

2. Click the Close (x) button at the right end of the title bar. The item disappears from your desktop.

To display a hidden item, follow these steps:

1. Right-click an empty spot on your desktop, and then point to Active Desktop.

2. Click Customize My Desktop.

3. On the Web tab, in the section Items on the Active Desktop, click to place a check mark in the box next to the item you want to display.

4. Click OK.

REMOVING A DESKTOP COMPONENT

To remove a Desktop Component, follow these steps:

1. Right-click an empty spot on your desktop.

2. Point to Active Desktop, and then click Customize My Desktop.

3. On the Web tab, in the section Items on the Active Desktop, click the item you want to remove; then click the Delete button.

4. A message box asks if you're sure you want to delete the item and its subscription. Click Yes.

5. Click OK to close the Display Properties dialog box.

 Subscriptions Subscriptions are what keep the information in each item updated; see Lesson 19, "Managing Subscriptions," to learn more about them.

In this lesson, you learned about Desktop Components—what they are, how to get more of them, and how to customize them. In the next lesson, you learn how to manage subscriptions.

MANAGING SUBSCRIPTIONS

In this lesson, you learn how to use subscriptions to download current information from your favorite web sites automatically.

WHAT ARE SUBSCRIPTIONS?

Subscriptions are a way to save time getting the Internet information you want. A subscription doesn't replace surfing or searching the web to locate information, but it automates the process of downloading from web sites current information that you read frequently, like an online magazine or newspaper. You can use a subscription to download newspaper stories, financial information, or sports scores while you're away from your computer (perhaps at lunch or overnight) and have the information waiting for you to read, offline and at your leisure, when you return.

Internet Explorer 4.0 uses a web crawling agent to go online at scheduled intervals, visit specific sites, check for changed information at each site, and then either download the new web pages or notify you that pages have changed so that you can choose which ones to download.

Web Crawling Agents A web crawling agent, or web crawler, is a software program that goes online to search out and download web sites and follow links to more web sites—all without your guidance or attention. It's like a robot Internet surfer.

SUBSCRIBING TO A SITE

To subscribe to a site, you must add it to your Favorites list, and then subscribe to it and set a schedule for the web crawler to check it for changed information. To subscribe to a site, follow these steps:

1. In your browser, open the web page you want to subscribe to.

2. In the browser window, click Favorites, and then click Add To Favorites.

3. In the Add Favorites dialog box (see Figure 19.1), click one of the following options:

   - Select Yes, but Only Tell Me When This Page Is Updated if you want to be notified of changes but don't want the pages downloaded automatically.

   - Select Yes, Notify Me of Updates and Download the Pages for Offline Viewing if you want to have changed pages automatically downloaded.

   If you check the latter option, your first wizard step asks whether you want to download this page only or all linked pages. Be careful about downloading all linked pages because you may end up downloading many megabytes of information.

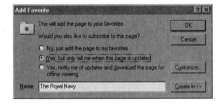

FIGURE 19.1   Subscribing to a new favorite.

4. Click Customize. The Subscription Wizard starts.

5. In the first wizard step, you can choose to be notified of changes via email. This is helpful if you're on the road with your laptop and checking in with your home-base computer. If you select the No option, a small red asterisk appears on the page icon in the Subscriptions dialog box to notify you of changes.

6. In the second wizard step, fill in any user name and password required by your subscribed site (if it's a site you normally have to log into with a password, the web crawler needs your password to check the site for you). Most web sites don't need passwords, however. Click Finish to complete your subscription.

7. Click OK to close the Add Favorites dialog box. The web page is added to your Favorites list and will be checked on the schedule you set. (See the following section, "Customizing Subscription Settings," for details on setting up a schedule.)

If the site is already on your Favorites list, follow these steps to subscribe:

1. In your browser window, click Favorites.

2. Right-click the site you want to subscribe to, and then click Subscribe.

3. Follow steps 5 through 7 of the preceding list to complete the subscription.

Customizing Subscription Settings

When a subscribed site has changed, your notification appears as a red asterisk on the page icon in your Subscriptions dialog box, like the ones shown in Figure 19.2. You can switch your subscription settings from mere notification to actually downloading the changed information, and you can change the site-checking schedule.

Icons with
red asterisks

FIGURE 19.2 Two of the subscriptions have changed contents, as indicated by the asterisks on their icons.

To switch your notification settings, follow these steps:

1. In your browser window, click Favorites, and then click Manage Subscriptions.

2. In the Subscriptions dialog box, right-click the web site you want to change, and then click Properties. The Subscription tab (see Figure 19.3) shows your current subscription settings.

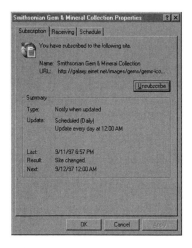

FIGURE 19.3 The Subscription tab, where you'll find your current settings.

CHANGING NOTIFICATION SETTINGS

On the Receiving tab (see Figure 19.4), you can change the settings for notification of site changes.

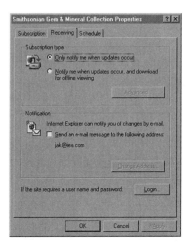

FIGURE 19.4 Set notification preferences on the Receiving tab.

These are the settings you can select on the Receiving tab:

- Be notified by email of changes in the web site. If you want to be notified by email, but at a different address, click the check box under Notification, and then click the Change Address button and type the address to which you want email notification sent.

- To select notification only, click the Only Notify Me When Updates Occur option. This option is much faster than actual automatic downloading and enables you to download the changed site separately from other subscribed sites.

- To direct the Web crawler to download the site automatically whenever it changes, click the Notify Me When Updates Occur and Download for Offline Viewing option. Then click the Advanced button to select download options from the Advanced Download Options dialog box.

- In the Advanced Download Options dialog box (see Figure 19.5), you can set a maximum size for downloads, and choose which types of page content to download (images, sounds, video, and so on). You can direct the web crawler to download only the subscribed page, or follow links on that page and download other pages within that web site (up to five levels deep). You also can have the web crawler follow links to pages outside the subscribed web site and download those pages. Be careful with this option, because you can easily fill your hard drive with downloaded web pages.

FIGURE 19.5   The Advanced Download Options for a specific site.

 TIP   **Links Don't Work in Downloaded Pages**   After the web crawler downloads a changed page, it disconnects itself from the Internet. So if you point to a link on a page you've downloaded, you'll see a *not* symbol (a circle with a diagonal slash). To follow the link, click the link, and then click the Connect button in the dialog box that appears. Your browser connects and opens the link.

Changing Schedule Settings

On the Schedule tab (see Figure 19.6), you can change the web crawler's update schedule.

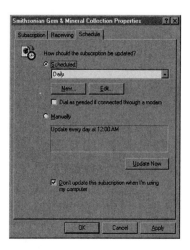

Figure 19.6 Set an update schedule on the Schedule tab.

The following are the settings you can select on the Schedule tab:

- **Scheduled** enables you to set a schedule for the web crawler to go online and check your subscribed sites for changed information (see Figure 19.7). You can set a daily, weekly, or monthly schedule, and set a time for downloads (overnight is a good choice if your web crawler will be downloading lots of information). You also can have the web crawler repeat the check at hourly intervals if you need to catch late-breaking news.

- **Manually** directs the web crawler to check for changes in a web site only when you tell it to do so, rather than automatically.

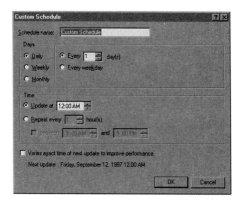

FIGURE 19.7   Set a custom schedule to check your subscribed sites.

DOWNLOADING SUBSCRIPTIONS NOW

If you have set your web crawler to the Manually schedule, you can send it online to download changed information whenever you choose. If you think it will be a long download, send the web crawler out before you go to lunch, and your new pages will be waiting for you when you return.

Even if you have your subscriptions set to download automatically, you can update them off-schedule whenever you want. This comes in handy if you're on your way out of town and want to check a subscribed site once more before you leave.

DOWNLOADING ALL YOUR SUBSCRIPTIONS

To download changed pages from all your subscribed sites at your command, follow these steps:

1. In the browser window, click Favorites.

2. Click Update All. The web crawler goes online and checks each of your subscribed pages for changes. A Download Progress message box appears while the web crawler is at work and disappears when the web crawler is finished.

Click the Details button to watch the progress of the downloads (see Figure 19.8). To stop the download at any point, click the Stop button in the Download Progress message box.

To skip downloading a specific site, click that site, and then click the Skip button.

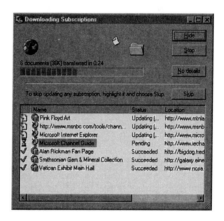

FIGURE 19.8   A subscription download in progress.

DOWNLOADING A SINGLE SITE

To download changed pages from a single subscribed site, follow these steps:

1. In your browser window, click Favorites, and then click Manage Subscriptions.

2. Right-click the site you want to check for updated information.

3. Click Update Now. The web crawler goes only to that site to check for changed pages. If there are changes in that site, a red asterisk appears on the icon, and you can open the page by double-clicking it.

Viewing a Changed Site

When changed information has been downloaded, follow these steps to view the downloaded page:

1. In the browser window, click Favorites.

2. Point to Subscriptions, and then click Manage Subscriptions.

3. In the Subscriptions dialog box, double-click the page you want to read.

Deleting a Subscription

To unsubscribe to a site, follow these steps:

1. In your browser window, click Favorites.

2. Right-click the site you want to unsubscribe, and click Unsubscribe.

3. In the Confirm Item Delete message box, click Yes. Your subscription is canceled, but the site remains on your Favorites list so that you can visit it when you want.

In this lesson, you learned about Subscriptions and how you can use them to download current information from the web automatically. In the next lesson, you learn how to manage Internet Explorer 4.0's new Channel feature.

MANAGING CHANNELS

In this lesson, you learn what channels are, how to subscribe to them, and how to organize and update them.

WHAT ARE CHANNELS?

Channels are web sites that come to your computer the way television channels come to your television set. They are a specialized form of subscription to web sites. You cannot navigate to a channel by typing a URL in your browser; but after you subscribe to a channel, you can view it in your browser window by clicking a channel button on the Channel bar.

If your computer is on a network that has constant Internet access (a constant open line to the Internet so that channels can *push* information into the network), any channel you subscribe to is automatically updated by the channel's provider and you simply open the channel on your computer to see the latest information. If your computer isn't on a network, channels work like subscriptions—you update them manually or on a web crawler schedule to get the latest information.

Internet Explorer 4.0 comes with built-in access to many channels, but as time goes by more channels will no doubt become available on the Internet, and you will be able to add them to your Channel Guide.

USING CHANNELS

You can open a channel from the Channel Guide desktop component on your Active Desktop (if you have the Active Desktop turned on), from the Channel bar in your browser window, from the list of channels in the Channels folder on your Favorites menu, or from the Channel Guide in the Channel Viewer.

The Channel Viewer is a full-screen view of your browser window, with toolbars along the top of the screen that AutoHide, and the Channel Guide on the left side of the screen that also slides out of view. The Channel Viewer gives you an unimpeded view of the web channel (or any other web site you navigate to).

To switch between Channel View and a normal browser window view, click View, and then click Full Screen. In this chapter, you see channel information demonstrated using the Channel Viewer.

 TIP **See Other Programs Without Switching to the Browser Window** You can view other open programs on top of the Channel Viewer by pressing Alt+Tab (press the Alt key and the Tab key simultaneously). A small dialog box appears that contains icons for each open program—hold down the Alt key and press the Tab key repeatedly to cycle through the icons. When the icon for the program you want has the selection border around it, release the Alt and Tab keys. The selected program appears on top of the Channel Viewer window.

To use the Channel Viewer, follow these steps:

1. On the Quick Launch toolbar, click the View Channels button. The Channel Viewer launches (see Figure 20.1).

2. If the Channel Guide isn't in view on the left side of the screen, move the mouse pointer to the left edge of your screen. The Channel Guide slides into view, and slides out of view when you move the mouse pointer away.

3. If the menu bar and toolbars remain in view at the top of the screen, right-click the menu bar, and then click AutoHide. The menu bar and toolbars slide out of view until you point at the top of your screen. When all the accessory bars are out of view and a channel is open, the Channel Viewer looks like Figure 20.2.

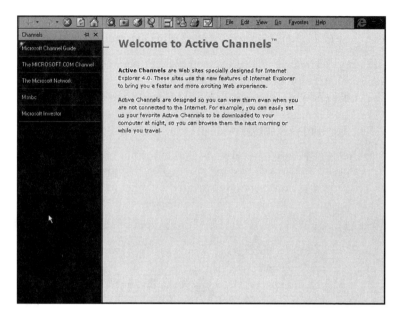

FIGURE 20.1   The Channel Viewer, a full-screen view of your browser window.

TIP   **Make the Channel Guide Narrower**   To make the Channel Guide narrower (or wider), point to the right edge of the Channel Guide until you see a two-headed arrow, and then drag the edge to the width you want.

USING THE CHANNEL GUIDE

The Channel Guide is like the remote control for a television set: You click a button to open a channel and see what's on. The Channel Guides (on the Active Desktop and the Channel Viewer) and the Channel bar (in a browser window) work the same way.

The first time you open a channel, you get a preview of what the channel offers and the opportunity to subscribe. After you subscribe, you get the latest information on the channel.

FIGURE 20.2   The Channel Viewer in full, unimpeded glory.

To open a channel, click a button (a rectangle) on the Channel Guide. If your computer is on a network that's online, the channel opens. If you haven't subscribed to the channel, Internet Explorer dials up the web site so that you can see a preview and subscribe.

SUBSCRIBING TO CHANNELS

When you preview a channel, the channel provider gives you the opportunity to subscribe. The subscription button is a bit different on each channel because it's provided by the individual channel, but each channel uses the Channel Subscription Wizard to guide you through the process of subscribing.

To subscribe to a channel, follow these steps:

1. Click the channel button or link in the Channel Guide to open the channel preview. Internet Explorer dials up the channel.

2. On the preview page, click the button, graphic, or link that indicates subscription (such as the Add Our Channel graphic). The Modify Channel Usage dialog box appears (see Figure 20.3).

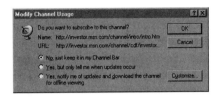

FIGURE 20.3   The Modify Channel dialog box, with default
subscription settings.

3. Choose one of the following options from the Modify
   Channel Usage dialog box:

   - **No, Just Keep It in My Channel Bar.** If you
     choose this option, a button is added to the Chan-
     nel bar; you can click that button to open the chan-
     nel, but the channel is not checked for changes
     automatically.

   - **Yes, but Only Tell Me When Updates Occur.** If
     you select this option, the channel is checked for
     changed information, and a red asterisk appears on
     the channel's icon in the Subscription dialog box
     when the channel has new information (but the
     changed pages are not downloaded).

   - **Yes, Notify Me of Updates and Download the
     Channel for Offline Viewing.** If you choose this
     option, changed pages are automatically down-
     loaded on the schedule you set so that you can open
     the pages and read them offline.

   Which option you choose determines which questions
   the Subscription Wizard asks in the next few steps.

4. Click Customize, and the Subscription Wizard starts. Suppose you select Full Subscription. In the first wizard step,
   select how much new information you want to have
   downloaded automatically. If you download only the
   home page, you can go online later to follow the links
   that interest you. Click Next.

5. In the second wizard step, you can choose to be notified
   via an email message of changes in the channel. If you

choose Yes, you can change the email address by clicking the Change Address button. After you select an option, click Next or Finish. (If you choose notification only, you are finished with the wizard; if you choose to have content downloaded, continue to the next step.)

6. In the third wizard step, choose a site-checking schedule. You can choose to update Manually or to use a Scheduled Update. Click the New button to set a schedule.

7. In the Custom Schedule dialog box (see Figure 20.4), set a schedule for your computer to check the channel site. Keep in mind that if you set a schedule for midnight every night (which is convenient because you probably won't be using the computer at that time), the computer must be left on so that Internet Explorer can dial into the channel.

8. In the Custom Schedule dialog box, click OK. Next, click Finish in the wizard step. Finally, click OK in the Add Channel dialog box, and your subscription is complete. To update immediately, right-click the channel name in the Channel Guide and click Update.

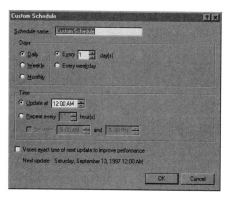

FIGURE 20.4   Set a custom schedule for channel checking.

Updating Channels

If your computer is on a network, you don't need to update channels because you'll always find the most current information on the channel when you open it. If you're using a standalone computer and you've set a manual update schedule, you'll need to direct the computer to go online and check your channels for new information. If you're headed out of the office and want to check a channel for fresh information one last time before you go, you can update manually instead of waiting for the next scheduled update.

To update a specific channel manually, follow these steps:

1. In the browser window, click Favorites, and then click Manage Subscriptions.

2. In the Subscriptions dialog box (see Figure 20.5), right-click the channel you want to update and click Update Now. Internet Explorer goes online to check the channel for changes and either notifies you of changes or downloads the site, depending on your subscription settings.

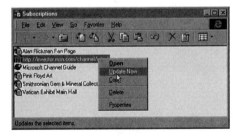

Figure 20.5   In the Subscriptions dialog box, channel icons are different from subscribed-site icons.

To update all channels manually, follow these steps:

1. In the browser window, click Favorites.

2. Click Update All Subscriptions. Internet Explorer goes online to check all subscribed sites and channels for changes and either notifies you of changes or downloads pages, depending on your subscription settings for each subscribed site or channel.

CHANGING A CHANNEL'S SUBSCRIPTION SETTINGS

If you change your mind about what you want downloaded and when, you can change the settings that you originally set in the wizard. To change a channel's subscription settings, follow these steps:

1. In any Channel Guide or Channel Bar, right-click the channel or channel folder you want to change.

2. Click Properties.

3. On the Receiving tab, set options for what you want downloaded.

4. On the Scheduling tab, set a schedule for updating or downloading.

5. Click OK to close the Properties dialog box.

DELETING A CHANNEL

There are bound to be channels you don't want in your channel guide. You can get rid of the visual clutter by deleting channels. To delete a channel, follow these steps:

1. In any Channel Guide or Channel bar, right-click the channel or channel folder you want to delete.

2. Click Delete. In the Confirm Folder Delete dialog box, click Yes. The folder or channel is removed to the Recycle Bin, so you can get it back if you change your mind.

If the channel was an unsubscribed button in the Channel Guide, you're finished. Close the Subscriptions dialog box.

If the channel was one you had subscribed to, you need to delete the subscription from the Subscriptions dialog box. Continue with step 3.

3. In a browser window, click Favorites. Point to Subscriptions, and then click Manage Subscriptions.

4. In the Subscriptions dialog box, right-click the subscription you want to delete, and then click Delete.

5. Close the Subscriptions dialog box.

In this lesson, you learned about using and managing specialized subscriptions called Channels. In the next lesson, you learn about add-ons, plug-ins, and helper applications that you can use to enhance your Internet Explorer web browser.

Using Add-Ons and Plug-Ins

In this lesson, you learn about web browser add-ons and plug-ins, and how you can use them to enhance Internet Explorer's capabilities.

Enhancing Your Web Browser's Capabilities

Internet Explorer provides you with a robust, full-featured web browser. It's great for surfing the World Wide Web, searching for your favorite web sites, and downloading great files and software. Believe it or not, you can extend and enhance the capabilities of Explorer with browser add-ons and plug-ins (a third enhancement possibility—ActiveX Controls—is covered in Lesson 22).

Add-ons and plug-ins can function as Explorer enhancers, increasing the capabilities of the browser. They can also function as helper applications to provide support for things that Explorer cannot do, such as view certain file types or play certain types of web files—for example, sound, video, and multimedia files—within the browser window.

Browser Add-On   A mini-program that runs in conjunction with the browser and supplies you with additional Internet tools, such as a special communication interface like Microsoft NetMeeting.

Plug-In A mini-program that usually provides your browser with the capability to play special content in the web browser window, such as certain video, audio, and multimedia files.

Add-ons and plug-ins can do a variety of things. For instance, add-ons such as NetMeeting and Microsoft Chat enhance Explorer's communication capabilities. Both add-ons provide you with the ability to communicate in real time with other users on the World Wide Web. Other add-ons and plug-ins, such as DirectShow, ShockWave (see Figure 21.1), and RealPlayer, help Internet Explorer play video, audio, and multimedia files you can find on the web.

Figure 21.1 Some add-ons and plug-ins such as ShockWave enable you to play special web files in the browser window.

TIP   **Plug-In Evolution**   At one time, plug-ins were strictly associated with the Netscape Navigator Web browser. Plug-ins have now become synonymous with any program that helps your web browser play special content within the browser window.

You will also come across add-ons and plug-ins that function outside of Internet Explorer as self-contained mini-programs. Microsoft DirectShow (see Figure 21.2) and NetShow play special web files in special players outside of the Explorer Window.

FIGURE 21.2   Some add-ons and plug-ins such as DirectShow play special web files outside the browser window.

Microsoft FrontPage Express is an Explorer add-on that provides you with an HTML editor you can use to design your own web pages. Web Server add-ons such as the Microsoft Publishing Wizard and the Personal Web Server help you publish your FrontPage Express content and get it onto the web.

POPULAR EXPLORER ADD-ONS

Microsoft offers several excellent add-ons for Internet Explorer. These add-ons range from the highly visual and fun Microsoft Chat to Microsoft Wallet, an add-on you can use with your Explorer Web browser to make secure purchases over the Internet.

As far as Explorer add-ons go, which ones you need depends on the type of Explorer installation you performed. When you use Active Setup to download the files for Internet Explorer 4.0, you're given the option of three different installations:

- Minimal (14M) includes Internet Explorer 4.0, Java Support, and the Microsoft Internet Connection Wizard.

- Standard (15M) adds Microsoft Outlook Express and Microsoft Wallet to the Minimal installation.

- Full (22M) adds Microsoft NetMeeting, NetShow, FrontPage Express, Microsoft Web Publishing Wizard, and Microsoft Chat 2.0 to the Standard installation.

Can't remember which installation you used? No problem; Microsoft offers a special Active Setup page for the various Internet Explorer add-ons that actually can tell you which components you have installed. Just do the following:

1. Connect to your Internet service provider or online service and open Internet Explorer.

2. In Internet Explorer's Address Box, type **www.microsoft.com/ie/ie40/download/b2/x86/ en/download/addon95.htm** and press Enter.

3. The Explorer components download page opens. The page asks you to wait while initialization takes place. The Active Setup dialog box appears and asks you whether you want it to determine which Explorer components are installed on your computer, as shown in Figure 21.3.

4. Click Yes to continue. Active Setup determines the status of each Explorer add-on component listed on the page. Add-ons already installed on your computer are marked "Already Installed" in the status area to the right of the particular component's name.

After you determine which add-ons aren't installed on your computer, you can use this web page to select and install them. For more information about downloading and installing a particular Explorer add-on, see the specific chapter that covers it.

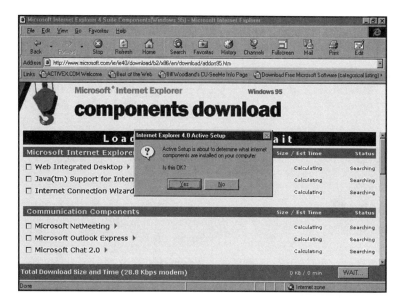

FIGURE 21.3 The Internet Explorer components download page will help you determine which Explorer add-ons you currently have installed.

A list of popular Internet Explorer add-ons appears Table 21.1.

TABLE 21.1 POPULAR INTERNET EXPLORER ADD-ONS

ADD-ON	DESCRIPTION
Microsoft NetMeeting	A communications program that provides an online environment for meetings. NetMeeting enables users to send audio and video information and communicate via an online Whiteboard.

continues

Table 21.1 **Continued**

Add-On	Description
Microsoft Outlook Express	The email client software for Internet Explorer 4.0. Refer to Chapter 12 for all the ins and outs of Outlook Express.
Microsoft Chat	A fun chat environment that you can use to "talk" to other users in real time.
Microsoft NetShow	A multimedia tool that enables you to send or view online multimedia presentations.
DirectX	A multimedia add-on that provides support for highly graphical web environments and DirectX games.
Microsoft FrontPage Express	A web design tool that enables you to create your own web pages.
Microsoft Publishing Wizard	A tool that helps you publish your web pages on a computer network that uses Microsoft NT Server and the Internet Information Server software.
Personal Web Server	This web publishing tool enables you to turn any computer into a web server so that others can access your web pages.
Microsoft Wallet	A utility program that provides you with an easy and secure way to pay for online transactions over the web.
Task Scheduler	An add-on that schedules common Windows maintenance programs, such as ScanDisk and Disk Defragmenter, and runs them automatically.

POPULAR EXPLORER PLUG-INS

Plug-ins also are a great way to enhance the capabilities of Internet Explorer. A number of popular plug-ins are described in Table 21.2.

TABLE 21.2   POPULAR EXPLORER PLUG-INS

PLUG-IN	DESCRIPTION
ActiveMovie	Microsoft's entry in the special web content player category, ActiveMovie enables you to play audio and video files in a number of different formats.
ShockWave	Used to view and interact with special multimedia web content that has been created in Macromedia Director or AuthorWare and then "shocked" for the web.
RealPlayer	Access tons of web audio and video using this popular player tool, including live broadcasts.
Apple QuickTime	Plays QuickTime movies from the web. QuickTime is one of the most popular formats for web video files.

FINDING ADD-ONS AND PLUG-INS

A number of web sites provide you with a library of Explorer add-ons and plug-ins. Because new add-ons and plug-ins are created constantly (sometimes there seems to be a total flood of new add-ons and plug-ins for a web browser), it pays to check these sites periodically to see what new items have become available.

Obviously, the first place to check for new add-ons and news about Microsoft Internet Explorer 4.0 is its page at the Microsoft web site. The address is **http://www.microsoft.com/ie4/**.

Other sites provide add-on and plug-in libraries. Stroud's Consummate Winsock Applications has a huge library of Internet-related software. The add-ons and plug-ins on the site are updated often. The address for Stroud's is **http://cws.internet.com/**.

Another great site is TUCOWS—The Ultimate Collection of Winsock Software. TUCOWS has many mirror sites that you can use to download Internet-related files, such as web browser plug-ins. The main TUCOWS site is at **http://www.tucows.com**.

Another site where you can find plug-ins and add-ons and tons of other shareware and freeware is **shareware.com**. This site has a huge library of all the latest and greatest software available on the web. You can connect to this site at **http://www.shareware.com**.

TIP   **Internet Search Engines**   You also can use any of the Internet search engines, such as Yahoo! (**www.yahoo.com**) and WebCrawler (**www.Webcrawler.com**), to find additional Explorer add-ons and plug-ins.

In this lesson, you became familiar with Internet Explorer add-ons and plug-ins—software programs that enhance and add to the capabilities of the Explorer web browser. In the next lesson, you learn about ActiveX controls, another great way to extend the capabilities of Internet Explorer.

USING ACTIVEX CONTROLS

In this lesson, you learn about ActiveX controls and how you can use them to expand the capabilities of the Internet Explorer Web browser.

UNDERSTANDING ACTIVEX CONTROLS

ActiveX controls supply you with another avenue for playing special web files or running mini-applications inside the Internet Explorer window. ActiveX technology is not unlike the object linking and embedding (OLE) technology that you use to link and share information between applications in the Windows environment. A specific ActiveX control links Internet Explorer to specific content or information in a special environment—the World Wide Web.

The ActiveX controls you install link Internet Explorer to the various helper applications that play the special web content files or run certain mini-applications. It is the ActiveX control that turns the Internet Explorer into a container where the special web content is seen or mini-applications are played.

ActiveX controls come in three types: controls that help the web browser play special content, controls that run mini-programs on the web, and special controls that are used by web developers. For end-users like you and me, the first two types of controls are the most important.

The ActiveX control for Adobe Acrobat is a good example of a control that's used to access special web content. Acrobat enables you to view special Acrobat files, which are desktop published document files (.pdf files) used for many online manuals (see Figure 22.1). Acrobat files are often used because they can easily display special text formatting and graphics that would be difficult using HTML.

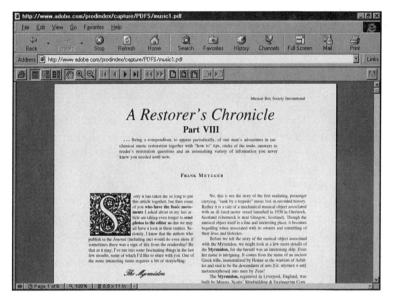

Figure 22.1 The ActiveX control for Adobe Acrobat allows you to open Acrobat files you find on the web.

An example of another mini-application that plays special content in the browser window is the VRML ActiveX Control. This control enables you to navigate three-dimensional worlds inside the Internet Explorer window (see Figure 22.2).

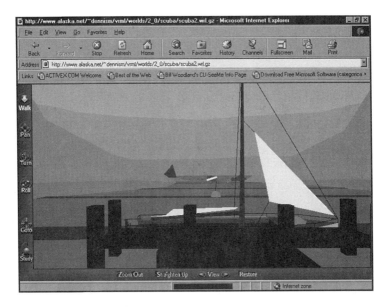

FIGURE 22.2   The VRML ActiveX Control works with Internet
Explorer to place you in three-dimensional web worlds.

POPULAR ACTIVEX CONTROLS

A large number of ActiveX controls already exist for Internet Explorer. Some of the most popular controls are listed in Table 22.1

TABLE 22.1   ACTIVEX CONTROLS

CONTROL	FUNCTION
VRML ActiveX Control	Enables you to explore three-dimensional web sites and objects by using Internet Explorer.
Adobe Acrobat	Enables you to access special desktop published web content in the form of Adobe Acrobat files.

continues

Table 22.1   Continued

Control	Function
ichat	Turns the Internet Explorer window into a real-time chat environment.
ActiveX Uninstaller	Enables you to remove unwanted ActiveX controls from your Internet Explorer installation.
Citrix Winframe Control	Enables you to share Windows-based information over the World Wide Web.

Where to Find ActiveX Controls

New ActiveX controls seem to appear almost daily. Fortunately, several web sites are available that will help you keep up-to-date on your install base of ActiveX controls.

Microsoft provides an ActiveX site that serves as a good starting place in your search for ActiveX information and new and improved ActiveX controls. You can access this site at **http:// microsoft.com/activex/gallery**.

Two other sites definitely worth checking out are ActiveX.com at **http://www.activex.com** and SoftSeek at **http:// www.softseek.com/**. ActiveX.com houses a rapidly growing library of ActiveX controls that you can download. This site also provides excellent descriptions of the ActiveX controls that it houses. SoftSeek has a large library of ActiveX controls and gives you detailed descriptions of each control. There are numerous links for downloading the listed ActiveX, providing you with more than one avenue to get the control onto your machine.

ActiveX Control Files   TUCOWS and Stroud's also house libraries of ActiveX control files. For TUCOWS, use the site at **http://tucows.mcp.com/**. For Stroud's, go to **http://www.stroud.com**.

In this lesson, you found out what ActiveX controls are and where to find them on the web. You also had an opportunity to learn about some of the more popular ActiveX controls for Internet Explorer. In the next lesson, you learn about Microsoft NetShow, a tool for sending and receiving multimedia presentations over the Internet.

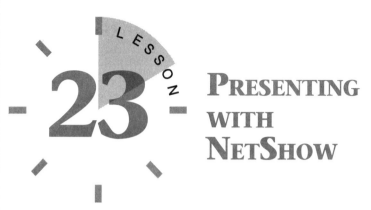

PRESENTING WITH NETSHOW

In this lesson, you download and install Microsoft NetShow. You also learn how to use NetShow to view multimedia presentations over the Internet.

INTRODUCING NETSHOW

Microsoft NetShow is an online multimedia presentation broadcaster. It enables you to view and develop web content that contains graphics, audio, video, and animation. Microsoft touts NetShow as the perfect tool for businesses and individuals who want to broadcast multimedia content over the web.

TIP

Further Information NetShow can be downloaded as a viewer, or you can download the NetShow server and tools software to develop your own multimedia content for the web. For more about these two NetShow items, check out **http://www.microsoft.com/netshow/**.

For end users like you, however, NetShow is more importantly a viewer and player that enables you to see and hear these web-based presentations. NetShow plays the multimedia content in streams, which means you don't have to wait for the whole presentation to download to your computer before it starts playing. This makes NetShow perfect for real-time presentations over the Net. NetShow presentations can even consist of synchronized audio and still pictures, making the old-fashioned slide show obsolete.

DOWNLOADING AND INSTALLING NETSHOW

NetShow is an add-on component for Internet Explorer and is available for download and installation from the Microsoft Internet Explorer Component Page.

1. Connect to the Internet and open Internet Explorer. In the address box, type **www.microsoft.com/ie/ie40/ download/b2/x86/en/download/addon95.htm** and press Enter.

2. The Internet Explorer Download page appears. The Active Setup box appears and asks whether you want to have the currently installed add-ons identified. Click Yes to continue.

3. Scroll down through the list of add-ons until you come to NetShow. Click its check box to select it for installation, as shown in Figure 23.1, and then click Next to continue.

4. The next page provides you with a drop-down box of download sites. Select the download site nearest you and click the Install Now button.

5. The Active Setup dialog box tracks the status of the download and installation process.

6. You are notified that the download and installation was a success (see Figure 23.2). Click OK to close the Active Setup notification box.

USING MICROSOFT NETSHOW

The NetShow player is now installed on your computer. NetShow can be used in two different ways. You can play NetShow files that have been stored on your computer, or you can play NetShow files and live content on the Internet.

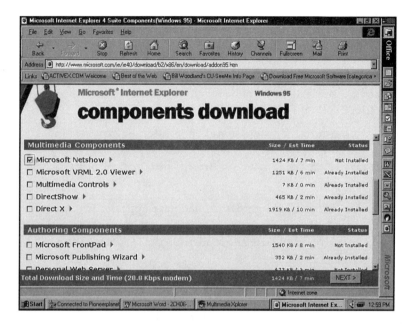

FIGURE 23.1   Click the NetShow check box and then click NEXT to have Active Setup download and install NetShow on your computer.

FIGURE 23.2   Active Setup lets you know that the download and installation of NetShow was a success.

PLAYING SAVED NETSHOW FILES

To play NetShow files that have been saved to your computer, NetShow is used like any other standalone audio or video player that you use in Windows. You start NetShow and then open the multimedia file (NetShow plays NetShow multimedia files only in the .asf and .asx format) you want to play.

To start NetShow and play a file on your computer, follow these steps:

1. Click the Start button, and then point at Programs. Point at the Internet Explorer group on the Program Menu.

2. Click the NetShow Player icon to start NetShow. The NetShow Player appears on your desktop, as shown in Figure 23.3.

FIGURE 23.3   NetShow can be used to play saved multimedia files that you store on your computer.

3. To open a saved multimedia file, click the File menu, and then click Open File.

4. In the Open dialog box, select the file and click Open. The presentation plays in the NetShow window, as shown in Figure 23.4.

FIGURE 23.4   NetShow plays presentation files in the NetShow window.

PLAYING NETSHOW PRESENTATIONS ON THE WEB

Although it may be useful to save NetShow presentations to your computer for later play, the real power of NetShow is playing presentations directly from the web. NetShow can play saved files on the web or play live content.

You will find that NetShow operates in much the same way that DirectShow does when you use it as an Internet Explorer helper application. When you click a link to multimedia files or a link to a live presentation, NetShow automatically starts, loads the content, and plays it for you.

One of the best places to find NetShow content is the NetShow Gallery at **http://www.microsoft.com/netshow/examples.htm**. This site contains examples of saved presentations and live presentations that you can play with NetShow.

Make sure you're online and have Internet Explorer open. Type **http://www.microsoft.com/netshow/examples.htm** in the Address box and then press Enter.

The NetShow Gallery page has a number of tabs that take you to pages containing links to NetShow content. You can choose from Samples, Live Events, Past Events, and Always Live events (see Figure 23.5).

You can do any of the following things:

- Click the Samples tab to check out some of the saved presentations that you can play with NetShow. The Samples include presentations on how to make espresso, how to get to Microsoft headquarters from the Seattle airport, and other presentations that show off NetShow's capability to deliver online multimedia content.

- Click the How To Make Espresso link. The NetShow window opens, and the espresso presentation is played.

- Click the Live Event tab, and you can view links to upcoming live broadcasts on a variety of subjects. The date and the time for a broadcast is included for your reference.

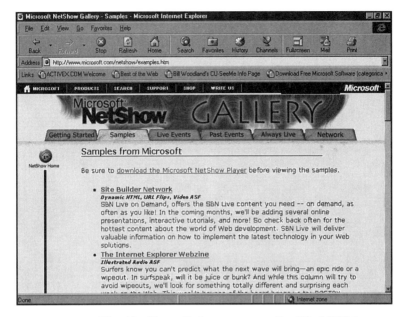

FIGURE 23.5   The NetShow Gallery page on the World Wide Web provides you with links to saved and live presentations that you can view with NetShow.

- If you can't wait for one of the live events, click the Always Live tab. This page gives you links to a number of broadcasts that are always live.

- Click the C-Span link on this page to get a live video feed from Capital Hill. When you click the link, you're taken to the AudioNet-sponsored C-Span page. A C-Span Online box in the center of the page contains the link to a live NetShow broadcast.

- Click the Click Here to View link. NetShow opens and provides a live video presentation from the C-Span network (see Figure 23.6). When you have finished viewing the live feed, click the NetShow Close button to close down the NetShow window.

The NetShow player provides you with an excellent tool for viewing all types of live and saved presentations. NetShow has the potential to become an exceptional educational delivery tool for Internet online courses.

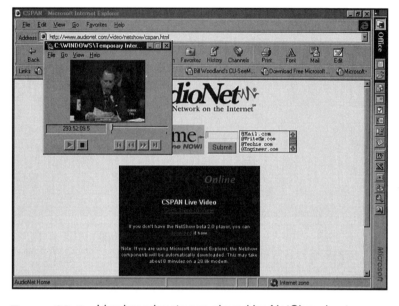

FIGURE 23.6 Live broadcasts are played by NetShow in streams, so you don't have to wait for large chunks of the broadcast to load before you see the video in the NetShow window.

In this lesson, you learned about Microsoft NetShow. You downloaded and installed the NetShow player and used it to play presentations on the World Wide Web. In the next lesson, you learn how to use NetMeeting.

CONFERENCING WITH NETMEETING

In this lesson, you learn how to place a conference call with NetMeeting, use the chat feature, and work with the Whiteboard.

PLACING A CONFERENCE CALL

NetMeeting, another one of the Internet Explorer 4.0 suite of programs, is a complete Internet conferencing system. NetMeeting capabilities include:

- Conferencing with up to 16 individuals via the Internet, using full-duplex audio and video.

- Text-based chat sessions permitting both group and individual messages.

- Sharing of applications between participants. For example, two (or more) grant writers could edit an application together in real time using Word 97.

- Visual collaboration through a shared whiteboard, allowing comments as well as graphics.

Full-Duplex The capability for a modem to conduct two-way conversations simultaneously. To check the capacity of your system, from the Tools menu, select Audio Tuning Wizard.

To set up an Internet conference call with NetMeeting, follow these steps:

1. Open Internet Explorer 4.0's File menu, select New, and then select Internet Call from the submenu. NetMeeting opens.

2. Click the Call button in the toolbar.

3. From the New Call dialog box, enter the email address, computer name, network address, or modem phone number of the person you want to call in the Address box. The Call Using box should be in the Automatic setting.

4. Click Call. NetMeeting finds the address you have called.

5. Click the Current Call tab on the left side of the screen.

6. When the connection is made, both your name and the name of the person you're calling appear in the Current Call window, as shown in Figure 24.1.

7. Speak into your computer's microphone. Adjust the sensitivity of the microphone and the volume of the speaker by moving the sliders on top of the window, if necessary.

8. To hang up the call, click the Hang Up button in the toolbar.

SENDING MESSAGES WITH CHAT

Chatting over the Internet is a very effective business tool for sharing ideas among wide-spread coworkers. Chatting is text-only and, although typing your thoughts may seem a limitation to those used to speaking them, it does overcome the limitations a slow network might bring to voice conferencing. Moreover, chat conferences can be saved and incorporated into any text document, such as an interview in a newsletter. To chat with someone using NetMeeting, follow these steps:

1. Open NetMeeting and call one or more individuals as described in the preceding task.

Microphone control   Whiteboard button
Call button   Chat button   Speaker control

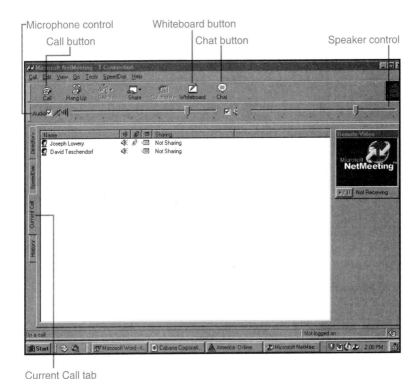

Current Call tab

FIGURE 24.1   Conference calling over the Internet with NetMeeting.

2. Click the Chat button in the toolbar. The Chat window opens (see Figure 24.2).

3. From the Chat window, type your text into the Message box. Press Enter to send the text. Your name appears next to your message in the main chat window.

4. To send a message to everyone in the chat session, make sure that Everyone in Chat appears in the Send To: box.

5. To send a private message, click the arrow next to the Send To: box to reveal the drop-down option list.

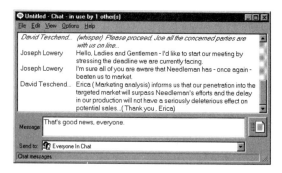

FIGURE 24.2 Chatting can be an effective business tool.

6. Click the name of the party to send your private message. Your message appears in italic as a "whisper" to the person indicated.

7. The main chat window scrolls as additional messages are added.

8. To save the entire chat, open the File menu, select Save, and enter the filename in the Save As dialog box.

9. To leave Chat, click the Close button in the Chat title bar.

INCORPORATING THE WHITEBOARD

A shared whiteboard allows team members to visually share their ideas and comments simultaneously—just as if they were all in the same conference room. NetMeeting's Whiteboard feature allows text, drawing, highlighting, and multiple pages. The Whiteboard can be combined with audio, video, and the Chat windows.To use the NetMeeting's Whiteboard, follow these steps:

1. Open NetMeeting and call one or more individuals as shown earlier.

2. Click the Whiteboard button in the toolbar. The Whiteboard window opens as shown in Figure 24.3.

Select Windows
button

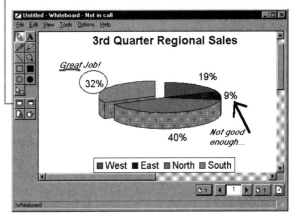

FIGURE 24.3   The Whiteboard allows visual collaboration.

3. From the Whiteboard window, select any of the various
   tools in the left toolbar. To use any of the drawing tools,
   select the button and drag into the main Whiteboard
   window to create the shape.

4. To move any object, click the Select tool and click and
   drag your object.

5. To put in text, click the Text tool, click the main
   Whiteboard window, and begin to type.

6. To add a page, click the Add a Page icon.

7. To insert a screen from another program, click the Select
   Window button and then click the screen to be inserted.

8. To leave the Whiteboard area, click the Close button in
   the Whiteboard title bar.

In this lesson, you learned how to place a conference call with
NetMeeting, use the chat feature, and work with the Whiteboard.
In the next lesson, you learn how to build a web page.

LESSON 25

BUILDING YOUR OWN WEB PAGE

In this lesson, you learn how to start FrontPage Express, format text, add graphics, save your web page and then browse it in Internet Explorer 4.0, and quit FrontPage Express.

STARTING FRONTPAGE EXPRESS

One of the reasons that the web has grown so rapidly is that web pages are easy to make. The language used to construct web pages, HTML, is easy enough to learn, but Internet Explorer 4.0 comes with its own editor that makes building web pages even easier. The program, FrontPage Express, is referred to as a WYSIWYG (What You See Is What You Get) editor, which means that you lay out your page just as you would in Publisher, and all the coding is handled behind the scenes. FrontPage Express is a separate program and can be started by following these steps:

1. Click the Start button on the taskbar.

2. Select Programs, and then from the submenu, select Internet Explorer Suite.

3. From the Internet Explorer menu, select FrontPage Express.

Figure 25.1 shows a FrontPage Express screen with a new, blank page, and highlights some of the key features.

FIGURE 25.1   FrontPage Express is Internet Explorer 4.0's editor.

FrontPage Express   You can also access FrontPage
Express through the Internet Explorer toolbar by clicking
Edit. This opens FrontPage Express and loads whatever
web page is currently open in Internet Explorer 4.0. Click
the New icon in the FrontPage Express toolbar to start
with a blank page.

FORMATTING TEXT

One main feature of a web page is its computer platform indepen-
dence. A web page built on a Windows 95 machine can be viewed
by Windows 3.1, Macintosh, UNIX, and any other system with a
basic browser. To reach this degree of universal accessibility, text
in web pages use formatting styles, such as STRONG or SMALL,
rather than specific font sizes as in a word processing program.

Headings, used for titles and subtitles, can be any one of six differ-ent relative sizes—Heading 1, the largest, through Heading 6, the smallest. Follow these steps to enter and format some text on your web page:

1. Start FrontPage Express.

2. Type in your first heading.

3. Select the text you just entered by clicking in front of it and dragging the mouse across the rest.

4. From the Change Styles box in the toolbar, click the ar-row to reveal the drop-down options list.

5. From the options list, click a text style choice. Heading 1 or Heading 2 is suitable for a web page title. The text changes to the selected size.

6. Keeping the text highlighted, click one of the Alignment buttons to make the text align to the Left, Centered, or Right.

7. If desired, click the standard Bold, Italic, or Underline style buttons.

8. Click anywhere on the blank page to clear the highlight.

Repeat these steps to continue to add text to your web page, vary-ing the text styles between Headings and Normal.

ADDING GRAPHICS

A major World Wide Web innovation was the inclusion of graph-ics with text. Most browsers currently support only two types of graphics. The first, GIF format, can have up to 256 colors and is used for drawings, logos, and illustrations. The second, JPEG, can display millions of colors but takes longer to load because it is compressed; JPEG is used primarily for photographs. Web graph-ics are in-line graphics, which means that they can be placed right next to text. Graphics can be aligned left, center, or right, just like text.

To place a graphic on your web page, follow these steps:

1. Move the insertion point to where you would like to have the graphic appear. If necessary, press Enter to move down the page.

2. From the Insert menu, select Image.

3. From the Insert Image dialog box, choose the Other Locations tab to select a graphic file from your hard drive or from a web address. Click OK when finished.

4. To select from one of the available clip art images, click the Clip Art tab and select a category. Click an image to select it, and then click OK.

5. The image is inserted on the page. To re-align the image, select it and click one of the Alignment buttons on the toolbar.

Figure 25.2 shows a web page with two lines of text and two images.

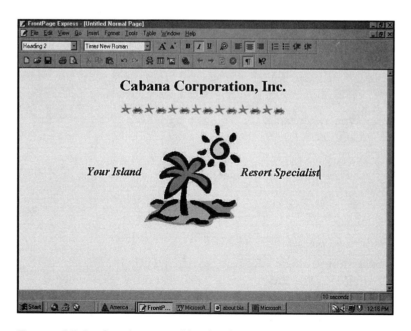

FIGURE 25.2   A web page with mixed graphics and text.

TIP **Re-use Graphics**   It's a good idea to re-use the same graphic image on the web site in several places. This gives continuity to a site with no additional download time. After a graphic has been downloaded, it is temporarily cached on the viewers system and can be re-used without re-downloading.

SAVING YOUR WEB PAGE

After you have spent some time creating your web page, you have to save it before you see it in Internet Explorer. Because web pages and web sites can be made of many separate files (each graphic is an individual file), you'll probably want to create a folder for each web site you work on. This also makes it easy to find all the files when it comes time to publish your creation to the web. FrontPage Express allows you to either publish directly to the Internet (or an internal intranet) or to a file. Follow these steps to save your web page as a file in FrontPage Express:

1. Click the Save button on the toolbar.

2. From the Save As Web dialog box, click the As File button.

3. Create a new folder, if necessary, from the Save As File dialog box by clicking the New Folder icon.

4. Type a new name for your web page in the Name box and click OK.

5. FrontPage Express asks whether you would like to copy your graphics to the new directory. Click the Yes To All button.

BROWSING YOUR WEB PAGE

You'll want to check your web page frequently in Internet Explorer. When you are browsing your creation, you can get an idea of how quickly (or how slowly) your page will load. You can also double-check your links and your graphics to make sure everything is in place. If you are eventually posting your page to the

Internet (as opposed to an internal network), look at your web page with different screen resolutions; you can't be sure what your potential readers are using, so it's best to see how your web page looks under a variety of circumstances. Follow these steps to browse a web page previously saved in FrontPage Express:

1. From the Internet Explorer File menu, select Open.

2. From the Open dialog box, click the Browse button.

3. Open the folder in which your web page is saved.

4. Double-click the file name of the web page you want to browse. The page loads and the dialog box closes.

 Fast Editing   When you are developing your web pages, keep both Internet Explorer 4.0 and FrontPage Express open. Move between the two by clicking the program's button on the taskbar. You can quickly see changes made in FrontPage Express by clicking the Refresh button in Internet Explorer.

QUITTING FRONTPAGE EXPRESS

When you have finished your FrontPage Express session, you quit the program by any of the standard methods:

- Choose File, Exit from the menu bar.

- Click the Close button in the upper-right corner of the FrontPage Express window.

- Use the keyboard shortcut, Alt+F4.

In this lesson, you learned how to start FrontPage Express, format text, add graphics, save your web page and then browse it in Internet Explorer 4.0, and quit FrontPage Express. In the next lesson, you learn how to publish your web page on the Internet.

26

PUBLISHING YOUR WEB PAGE

In this lesson, you learn how to place your page, its associated images, and other files on a web server.

After you have completed your web page, you must place it on a web server, where other people can open and view it with their web browsers. In the past, the only way to place a page on a web server was to use a separate FTP (File Transfer Protocol) program. However, FrontPage Express comes with its own file transfer program, called WebPost, that you can access simply by using the File, Save As command.

DEALING WITH THE PRELIMINARIES

Unless you've been working directly on a *web server* (a computer that stores web sites where people browsing the web can see them), you have to take the additional step of *publishing* your web pages.

Before you start, you need to make sure you have somewhere to store your web page. The best place to start is with your Internet service provider. Most providers make some space available on their web servers for subscribers to store personal web pages. Call your service provider and find out the following information:

- Does your service provider make web space available to subscribers? If not, maybe you should change providers.

- How much disk space do you get, and how much does it cost (if anything)? Some providers give you a limited amount of disk space, which is usually plenty for one or two web pages, assuming you don't include large audio or video clips.

- Can you save your files directly to the web server or do you have to upload files to an FTP server?

- What is the URL of the server you must connect to for uploading your files? Write it down.

- What username and password do you need to enter to gain access to the server? (This is typically the same username and password you use to connect to the service.)

- In which directory must you place your files? Write it down.

- What name must you give your web page? In many cases, the service lets you post a single web page, and you must call it **index.html** or **default.html**.

- Are there any other specific instructions you must follow to post your web page?

- After posting your page, what will its address (URL) be? You'll want to open it in Internet Explorer as soon as you post it.

If you're using a commercial online service, such as America Online or CompuServe, you may have to use its commands to upload your web page and associated files. For example, CompuServe has its own web page publishing wizard. In similar cases, you should use the tools the online service provides instead of trying to wrestle with FrontPage Express.

If your service provider doesn't offer web page service, fire up Internet Explorer, connect to your favorite search page, and search for places that enable you to post your web page for free. These services vary greatly. Some services require you to fill out a form, and then the service creates a generic web page for you (you can't use the page you created in FrontPage Express). At others, you can copy the HTML coded document (in Notepad or WordPad) and paste it in a text box at the site. A couple of other places let you send them your HTML file and associated files. Find out what's involved.

> **Preparing a Folder**   You can save yourself some time
> and trouble by placing your web page, all its graphic files,
> **TIP**   and any other associated files in a single folder separate
> from other files. The Web Publishing Wizard can then
> transfer all the required files as a batch to your web
> server. Make sure you use the correct filename for your
> web page file, as specified by your service provider.

SAVING YOUR PAGE TO A WEB SERVER

If you work on an intranet or use a service provider that enables you to save your web page directly to its web server, take the following steps to publish your web page:

1. Open the page you want to place on the web.

2. Open the File menu and select Save As. The Save As dialog box appears, displaying the name and location of your web page file.

3. Click OK. If you used any images or other files in your web page, a dialog box appears asking if you want to save these files to the web server (see Figure 26.1).

FIGURE 26.1   Be sure to save all associated files to the web server.

4. Click Yes to All. The Enter Network Password dialog box appears, prompting you to enter your username and password.

5. Type your username in the Username text box, tab to the Password text box, and type your password. Click OK. (FrontPage Express is set up to save your password, so you won't need to enter it the next time you publish a web page.)

6. The Web Publishing Wizard appears, displaying an explanation of what you are about to do. Click Next. The wizard prompts you to type a name for your web server.

7. Type a brief, descriptive name (you don't need to type the server's domain name at this point). Click Next. The wizard prompts you to type the URL of your web page.

8. Type the address of your web page, as specified by your service provider (for example, **http://www.internet.com/~bfink**). You may be prompted to enter your username and password again.

9. Click Next. The wizard prompts you to select your service provider, as shown in Figure 26.2. If you're unsure, select HTTP Post to place your files directly on a web server, or select Automatically Select Service Provider. Click Next. You are now prompted to enter information about the server.

10. Enter the server's name and any special command you need to upload your page to the web server. Your service provider should have supplied this information.

11. Click Next. The final dialog box appears, indicating that the wizard is ready to publish your web page.

12. Click Finish. The wizard dials into your service provider if you aren't yet connected and uploads your web page and all associated files to the web server. Dialog boxes appear, showing the progress.

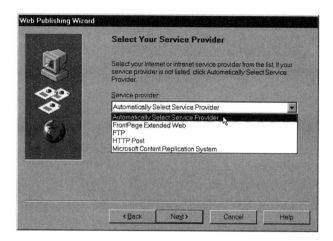

FIGURE 26.2   Select your service provider, or choose Automatically Select Service Provider.

Unable to Publish Files   If you receive an error message indicating that the wizard was unable to publish the files, you may have entered the wrong username or password, typed the wrong web server address, or selected the wrong service provider. Check with your service provider to ensure that you have the correct information and then repeat the steps.

Web Publishing Wizard   You also can run the Web Publishing Wizard by selecting Start, Programs, Internet Explorer, Web Publishing Wizard. When you run it this way, the steps are a little different. For example, the wizard enables you to upload an entire folder and all its subfolders to the server. If you have a complex collection of web pages, this can save you some time.

UPLOADING FILES TO AN FTP SERVER

Many service providers require that you upload your web page and associated files to an FTP server. When you open your account, the service provider creates a separate directory on the FTP server that only you can access using your username and password. You rarely deal with this directory, so you may not know its path. Ask your service provider to specify the path to your directory.

After you have the information you need, take the following steps to use the Web Publishing Wizard to upload files to your directory on the FTP server:

1. Open the page you want to place on the web.

2. Open the File menu and select Save As. The Save As dialog box appears, displaying the name and location of your web page file.

3. Click OK. If you used any images or other files in your web page, a dialog box appears asking if you want to save these files to the web server.

4. Click Yes to All. The Enter Network Password dialog box appears, prompting you to enter your username and password.

5. Type your username in the Username text box, tab to the Password text box, and type your password. Click OK. (FrontPage Express is set up to save your password, so you won't need to enter it the next time you publish a web page.)

6. The Web Publishing Wizard appears, displaying an explanation of what you're about to do. Click Next. The wizard prompts you to type a name for your web server.

7. Type a brief, descriptive name (you don't need to type the server's domain name at this point). Click Next. You may be prompted to enter your username and password again.

8. Type the address of your web page, as specified by your service provider (for example, **http:// www.internet.com/~bfink**). You may be prompted to enter your username and password again.

9. Click Next. The wizard prompts you to select your service provider.

10. Open the Service Provider drop-down list and select FTP, as shown in Figure 26.3. Click Next. You are then prompted to enter information about the server.

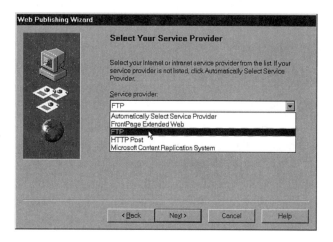

FIGURE 26.3   Select FTP as your service provider.

11. Enter the server's domain name (for example, **ftp.internet.com**) in the FTP Server Name text box.

12. Tab to the Subfolder Containing Your Web Pages text box, and type the path to the directory in which you must store your web pages (for example, **/users/bf/ bfink**) (see Figure 26.4). Your service provider should have supplied this information.

Specify the domain name   Type the path to the directory where
of your FTP server.   your web page files are stored.

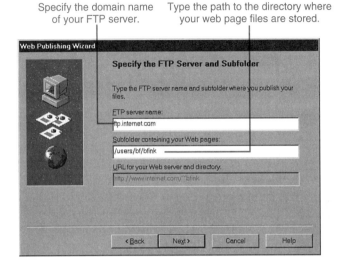

FIGURE 26.4   The wizard needs to know where to store your files.

13. Click Next. The final dialog box appears, indicating that the wizard is ready to publish your web page.

14. Click Finish. The wizard dials into your service provider if you aren't yet connected and uploads your web page and all associated files to the web server. Dialog boxes appear showing the progress.

TIP   **The Good News**   The good news is that you won't have to go through this 14-step process the next time you need to upload your web page. Simply choose the File, Save command, and FrontPage Express automatically uploads your web page and associated files to the FTP server.

In this lesson, you learned how to place your page and other files on the web.

INSTALLING INTERNET EXPLORER 4.0

Internet Explorer 4.0 is the latest version of Microsoft's Internet software. In addition to an upgraded World Wide Web browser, there are numerous other components that can be installed, including an Integrated Desktop that works with your Windows 95 desktop. For more information on the Integrated Desktop option, see Lesson 16, "Integrating the Web and the PC."

Follow these steps to install Internet Explorer 4.0:

1. Insert the Internet Explorer 4.0 CD-ROM into the appropriate drive.

   The first Internet Explorer 4.0 installation screen opens on your desktop automatically.

2. From the first installation screen, click the Install Internet Explorer 4.0 button.

3. The Internet Explorer 4.0 Active Setup window opens. When you're ready to proceed, click Next.

4. The Microsoft end-user license agreement appears on the next screen. After you have read the license, click the I Accept the Agreement box and then click Next.

5. The installation option screen appears, as shown in Figure A.1. Choose the installation option you prefer by clicking the drop-down arrow and selecting one of the following three choices:

   - **Minimal Installation** Installs only Internet Explorer and its multimedia plug-ins. If you are short of hard drive space, or if you already have an email and news client that you use, this is probably the best option for you.

- **Standard Installation**   Installs all of Internet Explorer and its multimedia plug-ins, Outlook Express for reading both email and news, and the Web Publishing Wizard. If you want to use Outlook Express for mail and news, you should choose this option.

- **Full Installation**   Installs all of Internet Explorer and its multimedia plug-ins, Outlook Express for reading email and news, Web Publishing Wizard, NetMeeting, FrontPage Express, and NetShow. This option is best if you want to do all your Internet exploration through the Microsoft Internet suite.

FIGURE A.1   You can choose from three different installation configurations.

6. Click Next.

7. On the next screen, you can choose to install the Integrated Desktop. Click Yes or No, and then click Next.

8. The Active Channel Selection screen provides you with a series of automatic business and entertainment channels that can be made available on your desktop. Select your country from the list, or choose another country that shares your language. Click Next when you're finished.

9. Select the location where you want the files installed. (The default is **c:\program file\internet explorer**.) Click Next.

10. Internet Explorer begins the preliminary installation process. A box details the progress of the installation. When completed, Internet Explorer asks you to close any open programs. Save all open documents and close all programs. Click Next on the Internet Explorer 4.0 Active Setup screen when you are finished.

    Internet Explorer needs to restart the computer to complete the installation.

After your computer is restarted, the setup continues. Various boxes, depending upon your installation choices, appear informing you of the progress.

When the installation is complete, if you have chosen to install Internet Explorer with the Integrated Desktop, your screen will look similar to Figure A.2.

FIGURE A.2   Internet Explorer's Integrated Shell enhances your desktop capabilities.

INDEX

SYMBOLS

" " (double quotes), web
searches, 19
* (asterisks), subscription
notifications, 133
+ (plus signs)
Outlook Express window,
94-95
web searches, 19
- (minus signs)
Outlook Express window,
94-95
web searches, 19

A

Accounts command (Tools
menu), Outlook Express, 80
Active Desktop, 111-116
background
HTML (web) documents,
113-114
Internet graphics,
115-116
pictures, 114-115
custom settings, 120

Desktop Components,
121-129
adding, 122-124
deleting, 128-129
Desktop Component
Gallery, 124
hiding/displaying, 128
moving, 125
resizing, 125
setting download
properties, 126
setting update schedules,
126-127
turning on/off, 121-122
updating now, 128
see also subscriptions
HTML layer, 116
see also Active Desktop,
Desktop Components
icon layer, 116
shortcuts, 117-119
arranging icons, 118
creating, 117-118
deleting, 119
opening programs/files,
117
single-click mode, 119
turning on/off, 113
Desktop Components,
121-122

Active Setup, Microsoft
NetShow add-on, 163-164
ActiveMovie (Microsoft)
plug-in, 155
ActiveX controls, 157-161
ActiveX Uninstaller, 160
Adobe Acrobat, 158
finding, 160
Start Page Stock Ticker, 47
VRML, 159
Add Favorite dialog box, 11-12
subscribing to sites, 131
add-ons, 149-156
determining installed
components, 152-153
finding, 155-156
installations, 151-153
Microsoft
DirectShow, 151
FrontPage Express, 151
NetMeeting, see
NetMeeting
NetShow, see NetShow
add-on
Outlook Express, see
Outlook Express
see also ActiveX controls;
plug-ins
Address Book (Outlook
Express), 57-58, 61-68
adding contacts, 63-64
LDAP directories, 62-63
adding groups, 65-67
addressing email, 57-58
deleting contacts, 67
editing contacts, 65
importing address books
old address books, 67-68
Outlook 97 books, 77-78
opening, 61
addresses
books, *see* Address Book
(Outlook Express)
domain names, 59

email addresses, 59-60
Internet directories, 61-63
Internet URLs (Universal
Resource Locators), 7-8
FTP sites, 30
Adobe Acrobat, 158
AltaVista search engine, 16
see also searches, search
engines
anonymous FTP sites, 29
Apple QuickTime plug-in, 155
asterisks (*), subscription
notifications, 133
attaching files to email, 56-57
AutoCompletion, entering
URLs, 8

B

Back/Forward buttons, 20
history lists, 10
backgrounds, Active Desktop
HTML (web) documents,
113-114
Internet graphics, 115-116
pictures, 114-115
see also wallpaper
BigFoot address directory, 61
browser display, customizing
colors, 48-49
disabling multimedia, 48
fonts, 49-50
browsing the web, *see*
navigating the web
buttons, *see* toolbars

C

cancelling downloads, 24
capturing web graphics, 25-27
certificates (security), 102-104
channels, 140-148
Channel Guide, 143
sizing, 142

Channel Viewer, 141-143
deleting, 147-148
opening, 143
scheduling site-checking, 145
subscribing, 143-145
changing subscription settings, 147
updating, 146-147
see also subscriptions
chat
ichat ActiveX control, 160
Microsoft Chat add-on, 154
NetMeeting chat, 170-172
Citrix Winframe Control (ActiveX), 160
closing
FrontPage Express, 179
Internet Explorer 4.0, 5-6
color, browser display, 48-49
commands
Active Desktop
Customize My Desktop, 122, 127-128
Update Now, 128
View As Web Page, 121
Address Book
Delete (File menu), 67
Find (Edit menu), 61-63
Import, Address Book (File menu), 68, 77
Favorites menu
Add To Favorites, 131
Manage Subscriptions, 133, 138, 146
Organize Favorites, 39
Unsubscribe, 139
Update All, 137
Update All Subscriptions, 147
File menu
Exit, 6
Page Setup, 36
Print, 36
Save As, 38
Work Offline, 34-35
Front Page Express, Image (Insert menu), 177
Outlook Express
Accounts (Tools menu), 80
Address Book (Tools menu), 63
Compact (File, Folders menu), 74
Compact All Folders (File, Folders menu), 73
Download All (Tools menu), 92
Import, Address Book (File menu), 77
Import, Messages (File menu), 76
Inbox Assistant (Tools menu), 71
Mail Options (Tools menu), 56
Move to Folder (Edit menu), 70
New Folder (File, New menu), 69
News (Go menu), 85
Newsgroups (Tools menu), 85-86
Print (File menu), 94
Retrieve (Tools menu), 54
View menu
Full Screen, 141
Internet Options, 48-50, 100, 103-104
compacting email folders, 73-74
composing/sending email messages, 52-54
Address Book, 57-58
attaching files, 56-57
priorities, 57

compressed files,
  decompressing, 24-25
conference calls, *see*
  NetMeeting
contacts (Address Book), 61
  adding, 63-64
    groups, 65-67
    Internet address
      directories, 61-63
  deleting, 67
  editing, 65
  importing address books
    old books, 67-68
    Outlook 97 books, 77-78
copying hypertext links, 27-28
Create Folder dialog box
  (Outlook Express), 69
creating web pages, *see*
  FrontPage Express
credit card security (Microsoft
  Wallet), 104-105
Custom Schedule dialog box
  (channels), 145
Custom Settings dialog box
  (Active Desktop), 120
customizing Internet Explorer
  4, 46-50
  Start Pages
    personalizing, 46-47
    selecting Start Pages,
      47-48
  web page display, 48-50
    colors, 48-49
    disabling multimedia, 48
    fonts, 49-50

D

decompressing files, 24-25
Deleted Items folder (Outlook
  Express), 73-74

deleting
  Address Book entries, 67
  channels, 147-148
  Desktop Components,
    128-129
  desktop icons, 119
  email messages, 73
    automatically, 74
  subscriptions
    (unsubscribing), 139
desktops
  Active Desktop, *see* Active
    Desktop
  shortcuts, *see* shortcuts
  wallpaper, *see* wallpaper
  Web Integrated Desktop,
    106-112
    Explorer bars, 110-111
    installing, 107
    removing, 107-108
    Standard toolbar,
      108-109
    Start menu, 110
    taskbar, 110
dialog boxes
  Active Setup (NetShow
    add-on), 163-164
  Add Favorite, 11-12
    subscribing to sites, 131
  Create Folder (Outlook
    Express), 69
  Custom Schedule
    (channels), 145
  Custom Settings (Active
    Desktop), 120
  Download File, 24
  Find People, 62
  Group Properties, 66
  Modify Channel Usage,
    143-145
  Newsgroups, 85-86
  Open (FTP sites), 30

Options
> *Advanced tab, 48-49*
> *Content tab, 103-104*
> *General tab, 50*
> *Send tab (Outlook*
>   *Express), 82*
> *Programs tab, 104-105*
> *Security tab, 100-102*
Organize Favorites, 39-41
Print, 36-37
Quick Link, 45
Save HTML Document, 38
Select Group Members, 67
Select Recipients, 58
Subscriptions
> *Advanced Download*
>   *Options tab, 134-135*
> *Receiving tab, 134*
> *Schedule tab, 136*
> *Subscription tab, 133*
DirectShow add-on, 151
DirectX add-on, 154
disabling multimedia, 48
display, customizing, 48-50
> colors, 48-49
> disabling multimedia, 48
> fonts, 49-50
displaying/hiding Desktop
  Components, 128
domain names, 59
double quotes (" "), web
  searches, 19
downloading
> ActiveX controls, 160
> add-ons/plug-ins, 155-156
> Desktop Components
>   *setting download*
>   *properties, 126*
>   *setting update schedules,*
>   *126-127*
>   *updating now, 128*
> files, 23-24
>   *cancelling downloads, 24*
>   *decompressing, 24-25*

FTP (File Transfer Protocol),
  29-30
> *opening FTP sites, 30*
> *retrieving files, 31-33*
graphics, 25-27
Microsoft NetShow, 163-164
newsgroups
> *message headers, 88-90*
> *tagged messages, 91-92*
subscriptions, 137-138
> *all subscriptions,*
>   *137-138*
> *following hypertext links,*
>   *135*
> *single sites, 138*
> *stopping downloads, 138*
> *viewing, 138-139*

E

Edit menu commands
> Address Book, Find, 61-63
> Outlook Express, Move to
>   Folder, 70
editing web pages, *see*
  FrontPage Express
email, 52-58, 69-74
> addresses, 57-60
>   *adding groups to Address*
>   *Book, 65-67*
>   *adding to Address Book,*
>   *63-64*
>   *deleting from Address*
>   *Book, 67*
>   *editing in Address Book,*
>   *65*
>   *importing old address*
>   *books, 67-68*
>   *importing Outlook 97*
>   *address books, 77-78*
>   *Internet directories, 61-63*
> attaching files, 56-57

composing/sending
 messages, 52-54
  priorities, 57
deleting messages, 73
  automatically, 74
legal considerations, 98
reading messages, 54
replying to messages, 55-56
retrieving messages, 54-55
sorting, 69
  compacting folders, 73-74
  creating folders, 69-70
  filtering incoming
   messages, 71-72
  importing Outlook 97
   folders, 76-77
  moving email into folders,
   70-71
Excite search engine, 16
see also searches, search
 engines
Exit command (File menu), 6
exiting
 FrontPage Express, 179
 Internet Explorer 4.0, 5-6
Explorer
 bars (Web Integrated
  Desktop), 110-111
 Favorites Explorer, *see*
  favorites, Favorites
  Explorer
 Search Explorer, 15-16
exploring web sites, 8-10
 Back/Forward buttons, 10,
  20

F

favorites, 11-12
 adding, 11-12
  subscribing to sites, 131
 Favorites Explorer, 42-43

Favorites menu commands
 Add To Favorites, 131
 Manage Subscriptions,
  133, 138, 146
 Organize Favorites, 39
 Unsubscribe, 139
 Update All, 137
 Update All Subscriptions,
  147
 organizing, 11-12, 39-41
 search categories, 20
 Start menu options (Web
  Integrated Desktop), 12
 subscribing to sites
  current favorites, 132
  new favorites, 131-132
  unsubscribing, 139
 updating, 137, 147
 viewing
  pages offline, 34-35
  thumbnails, 41-42
 visiting, 12
 see also subscriptions
File menu commands
 Address Book
  Delete, 67
  Import, Address Book,
   68, 77
 Exit, 6
 Outlook Express
  Folders, Compact, 74
  Folders, Compact All
   Folders, 73
  Import, Address Book, 77
  Import, Messages, 76
  New, New Folder, 69
  Print, 94
 Page Setup, 36
 Print, 36
 Save As, 38
 Work Offline, 34-35
File Transfer Protocol, *see* FTP

files
    attaching to email messages,
    56-57
    downloading, 23-24
        cancelling downloads, 24
        decompressing, 24-25
        see also downloading
    uploading (web pages)
        FTP servers, 185-187
        web servers, 182-184
filtering incoming email
    messages, 71-72
finding, *see* searches
folders
    Deleted Items (Outlook
    Express), 73
        emptying automatically,
        74
    email
        compacting, 73-74
        creating, 69-70
        importing from Outlook
        97, 76-77
        storing messages, 70-71
    Favorites, 11-12
    viewing thumbnails, 41
fonts, browser display, 49-50
formatting web page text,
    175-176
Forward/Back buttons, 20
    history lists, 10
Four11 address directory, 61
FrontPage Express, 174-179
    add-ons, 151
    closing (exiting), 179
    formatting text, 175-176
    placing graphics, 176-178
    saving web pages, 178
    starting, 174-175
    viewing web pages, 178-179
FTP (File Transfer Protocol),
    29-33
    anonymous logins, 29
    opening FTP sites, 30

    retrieving files, 31-33
    uploading web pages to FTP
    servers, 185-187
Full Screen command (View
    menu), 141

G-H

Go menu commands (Outlook
    Express), News, 85
graphics
    adding to web pages,
    176-178
    Active Desktop back-
    grounds, 115-116
    saving web graphics, 25-27
groups, creating (Address
    Book), 65-67

hiding/displaying Desktop
    Components, 128
history lists, 20-22
    Back/Forward buttons, 10
    clearing, 22
    setting days to keep history,
    22
home pages
    creating, *see* FrontPage
    Express
    Start Pages
        personalizing, 46-47
        selecting new Start Pages,
        47-48
        Stock Ticker, 47
HotBot search engine, 17
    see also searches, search
    engines
HTML (Hypertext Markup
    Language), 37
    Active Desktop HTML layer,
    116
        backgrounds, 113-114
    saving web pages, 37-38

hypertext links, 9
  copying/saving from web,
    27-28
  desktop shortcuts, 43-44
  downloaded subscription
    pages, 135
  following, 9-10
  Quick Links, 44-45

I

ichat ActiveX control, 160
icons, Active Desktop
  arranging, 118
  creating shortcut icons,
    117-118
  deleting, 119
  icon layer, 116
  opening programs/files, 117
  single-click mode, 119
images, *see* graphics; pictures
importing
  email address books, 67-68
    from Outlook 97, 77-78
  email message folders, 76-77
Inbox (Outlook 97), 76
Inbox Assistant (Outlook
  Express), 71
  filtering email, 71-72
InfoSeek search engine, 17
  see also searches, search
    engines
InfoSpace address directory, 61
Insert menu commands (Front
  Page Express), Image, 177
installing
  Internet Explorer 4, 188-191
    add-ons, 151-153
    choosing file locations,
      190
    installation options,
      188-189
    Integrated Desktop,
      190-191

Microsoft NetShow, 163-164
Web Integrated Desktop,
  107
Internet
  addresses
    domain names, 59
    email addresses, 59-60
    LDAP directories, 61-63
  Connection Wizard,
    configuring new servers,
    80-82
  Internet Options command
    (View menu), 48-50, 100,
    103-104
  searching, *see* searches
  security, *see* security
  service providers, *see* ISPs
  Zone, 100
    see also security, zones
  see also World Wide Web
Internet Explorer 4.0, 1-6
  closing/(exiting), 5-6
  installing, 188-191
    add-ons, 151-153
    choosing file location,
      190
    installation options,
      188-189
    Integrated Desktop,
      190-191
  screen layout, 3-4
  starting, 2-3
  toolbar, 4-5
  web page, 155
ISPs (Internet service
  providers), 79
  configuring news servers,
    79-82
  publishing web pages, *see*
    publishing web pages

J-K-L

keyboard shortcuts
   Address Book, 61
   Close (Internet Explorer), 6
   Find, 61
   New Contact, 63
   New Group, 65
   Print, 94
   Properties (contacts), 65
keywords, web searches, 19

LDAP (Lightweight Directory Access Protocol), 61
   address directories, 61-63
links
   hyperlinks, *see* hypertext links
   Links toolbar, adding Quick Links, 44-45
Local Internet zone, 100
   see also security, zones
Lycos search engine, 17
   see also searches, search engines

M

mail, *see* email
Manage Subscriptions command (Favorites menu), 133, 138, 146
Microsoft
   ActiveMovie plug-in, 155
   ActiveX Gallery web page, 160
   Chat add-on, 154
   DirectShow add-on, 151
   FrontPage Express add-on, 151
   Internet Explorer 4.0 web page, 155
   NetMeeting add-on, *see* NetMeeting

NetShow add-on, 154, 162-168
   downloading/installing, 163-164
   playing live web files, 166-168
   playing local files, 164-165
   web site, 162, 166-168
   Outlook Express add-on, *see* Outlook Express
   Publishing Wizard add-on, 154
   Wallet add-on, 154, 104-105
minus signs (-)
   Outlook Express window, 94-95
   web searches, 19
Modify Channel Usage dialog box, 143-145
moving
   Desktop Components, 125
   email to folders, 70-71
multimedia, disabling, 48
Museum of Modern Art web site, 10

N

navigating the web, 7-14
   Back/Forward buttons, 10, 20
   entering URLs, 7-8
   exploring web sites, 8-10
   favorites, 11-12
   hypertext links, 9-10
   stopping web pages, 14
   surfing, 13-14
NetMeeting, 169-173
   Address Book contact information, 64
   chatting, 170-172

Current Call window,
170-171
placing conference calls,
169-171
starting, 170
Whiteboard, 172-173
NetShow add-on, 154, 162-168
downloading/installing,
163-164
playing
live web files, 166-168
local files, 164-165
starting, 165
web site, 162
NetShow Gallery,
166-167
New Folder command (File
menu), Outlook Express, 69
newsgroups
configuring
message windows, 82-83
servers, 79-82
downloading
message headers, 88-90
tagged messages, 91-92
getting newsgroup lists,
83-84
printing messages, 93-94
reading messages, 92-93
following threads, 94-95
unsubscribed newsgroups,
86
replying to messages
entire newsgroup, 95-96
message author, 97-98
sorting newsgroup lists,
84-86
subscribing, 86-87
tagging messages for
download, 90-91

O

offline browsing, 34-35
online services, publishing
web pages, 181
opening
FrontPage Express, 174-175
FTP sites, 30
Internet Explorer 4.0, 2
NetMeeting, 170
NetShow, 165
Options dialog box
Advanced tab, 48-49
Content tab, 103-104
General tab, 50
Send tab (Outlook Express),
82
Programs tab, 104-105
Security tab, 100-102
Organize Favorites dialog box,
39-41
Outlook 97, 75-78
exporting
Address Book into
Outlook Express, 77-78
folders into Outlook
Express, 76-77
Inbox, 76
Outlook Express
Address Book, *see* Address
Book
importing items from
Outlook 97, *see* Outlook
97, exporting
Inbox, 54-55
mail, 69-74
Address Book, 57-58
attaching files, 56-57
compacting folders, 73-74
composing/sending email,
52-54

creating folders, 69-70
deleting messages, 73-74
filtering messages, 71-72
importing Outlook 97
    folders, 76-77
moving email into folders,
    70-71
Outbox, 54
priorities, 57
reading email, 54
replying to messages,
    55-56
retrieving email, 54-55
news
    configuring message
        windows, 82-83
    configuring servers, 79-82
    downloading message
        headers, 88-90
    downloading tagged
        messages, 91-92
    following message
        threads, 94-95
    getting newsgroup lists,
        83-84
    printing messages, 93-94
    reading messages, 86,
        92-93
    replying to author, 97-98
    replying to newsgroups,
        95-96
    sorting newsgroup lists,
        84-86
    subscribing to
        newsgroups, 86-87
    tagging messages for
        downloading, 90-91
Preview Pane, 54-55

P

Page Setup command (File
    menu), 36
passwords, FTP sites, 29-30
Personal Web Server add-on,
    154
pictures
    Active Desktop
        backgrounds, 114-115
    saving web graphics, 25-27
plug-ins, 149-151, 155-156
    finding, 155-156
    ShockWave, 150, 155
    see also ActiveX controls,
        add-ons
plus signs (+)
    Outlook Express window,
        94-95
    web searches, 19
Preview Pane, Outlook
    Express, 54-55
printing
    newsgroup messages, 93-94
    Print command (File menu),
        36
    web pages, 35-37
protocols
    FTP (File Transfer Protocol),
        see FTP
    LDAP (Lightweight
        Directory Access Protocol),
        61
        address directories, 61-63
publishing web pages, 180-187
    considerations, 180-181
    Microsoft Publishing Wizard
        add-on, 154
    online services, 181
    uploading pages
        FTP servers, 185-187
        web servers, 182-184
push technology, see
    subscriptions

Q-R

Quick Launch toolbar View Channels button, 141
Quick Link toolbar, hypertext links, 44-45
QuickTime plug-in (Apple), 155
quotes (" "), web searches, 19
reading
 email, 54
 newsgroup messages, 92-93
  following threads, 94-95
  unsubscribed newsgroups, 86
RealPlayer plug-in, 155
receiving
 email, 54-55
 subscription notifications, 134
removing Web Integrated Desktop, 107-108
replying
 email, 55-56
 newsgroup messages
  entire newsgroup, 95-96
  message author, 97-98
Restricted Sites zone, 100
 see also security, zones

S

saving
 hypertext links, 27-28
 NetMeeting chat, 172
 Save As command (File menu), 38
 web graphics, 25-27
 web pages, 37-38
  FrontPage Express, 178
  see also favorites;
  publishing web pages

scheduling
 channel site-checking, 145
 subscription downloads, 136-137
searches, 15-20
 conducting
  advanced searches, 18-19
  searching by category, 19-20
  simple searches, 16-18
 email address directories, 61-63
 history lists, 20-21
 indexes, *see* searches, search engines
 search engines, 15-19, 156, 160
  categories, 19-20
 Search Explorer, 15-16
security, 99-105
 certificates, 102-104
 Microsoft Wallet, 104-105
 zones, 99-102
  assigning web sites, 101-102
  setting levels, 100-101
selecting
 group members, 67
 recipients, 58
sending email messages, 52-54
 Address Book, 57-58
 attaching files, 56-57
 replies, 55-56
 setting priorities, 57
servers
 configuring news servers, 79-82
 FTP (File Transfer Protocol), 29
 Personal Web Server add-on, 154
 uploading web pages
  FTP servers, 185-187
  web servers, 182-184

setup, *see* installing, Internet Explorer 4

shareware.com web site, 156

shell integration, *see* Web Integrated Desktop

ShockWave plug-in, 150, 155

shortcuts (desktop)
Active Desktop, 117-119
arranging icons, 118
creating, 117-118
deleting, 119
opening programs/files, 117
single-click mode, 119
hypertext links, 43-44

single-click mode (Active Desktop), 119

SoftSeek ActiveX web site, 160

Standard toolbar, Web Integrated Desktop, 108-109

Start menu, Web Integrated Desktop, 110
Favorites option, 12

Start Pages
personalizing, 46-47
selecting new Start Pages, 47-48
Stock Ticker, 47

starting
FrontPage Express, 174-175
Internet Explorer 4.0, 2-3
NetMeeting, 170
NetShow, 165
searches, 16

Stock Ticker (Start Page), 47

stopping web page transfers
downloads, 24
Stop button, 14

Stroud's web site, 160

subscriptions, 130-139
channels, 143-145
changing subscription settings, 147
updating channels, 146

deleting (unsubscribing), 139
downloading, 137-138
newsgroups, 86-87
settings
channels, 147
notifications, 132-135
schedules, 136-137
subscribing to sites, 131-132
viewing updated sites, 139
hypertext links, 135
see also channels; desktop components

Subscriptions dialog box
Advanced Download Options tab, 134-135
Receiving tab, 134
Schedule tab, 136
Subscription tab, 133

surfing the web, 13-14
see also navigating the web

Switchboard address directory, 61

T

tagging newsgroup messages for download, 90-91

Task Scheduler add-on, 154

taskbar
Surface/Restore Desktop icon, 44
Web Integrated Desktop, 110

text formatting, web pages, 175-176

thumbnails
favorites, 41-42
folders, 41

toolbars
Back/Forward buttons, 20
history lists, 10

Explorer bars (Web
    Integrated Desktop),
    110-111
  Favorites button, 11
  History button, 20-21
  Internet Explorer main
    toolbar, 4-5
  Links, adding Quick Links,
    44-45
  Mail button, 52, 54, 57
  moving/resizing, 4
  Quick Launch, View
    Channels button, 141
  Quick Links, hypertext
    links, 44-45
  Search button, 16, 18
  Standard toolbar (Web
    Integrated Desktop),
    108-109
  Stop button, 14
Tools menu commands
  (Outlook Express)
  Accounts, 80
  Address Book, 63
  Download All, 92
  Inbox Assistant, 71
  Mail Options, 56
  Newsgroups, 85-86
  Retrieve, 54
Trusted Sites zone, 100
  see also security, zones
TUCOWS web site, 156

U-V

Unsubscribe command
  (Favorites menu), 139
unzipping (decompressing)
  files, 24-25

updating
  channels, 146-147
  Desktop Components
    setting update schedules,
    126-127
    updating now, 128
  subscriptions, 137-138
    following hypertext links,
    135
uploading web pages
  FTP servers, 185-187
  web servers, 182-184
URLs (Universal Resource
  Locators), 7
  entering, 7-8
    AutoCompletion, 8
  FTP sites, 30
  hypertext links, *see*
    hypertext links
  saving, *see* favorites

viewing
  channels (Channel Viewer),
    141-143
  thumbnail favorites, 41-42
  View menu commands
    Full Screen, 141
    Internet Options, 48-50,
    100, 103-104
  web pages
    customizing display,
    48-50
    FrontPage Express,
    178-179
    offline browsing, 34-35
    printing, 35-37
VRML ActiveX control, 159

W

Wallet (Microsoft) add-on,
   104-105, 154
wallpaper (desktop), 112
   Active Desktop backgrounds
      HTML (web) documents,
         113-114
      Internet graphics,
         115-116
      pictures, 114-115
      setting from web, 112
   see also backgrounds
Web Integrated Desktop,
   106-112
   Active Desktop, 111-112
      see also Active Desktop
   Explorer bars, 110-111
      see also Explorer bars
   installing, 107
   removing, 107-108
   Standard toolbar, 108-109
   Start menu, 110
   taskbar, 110
Web Publishing Wizard,
   uploading pages
   FTP servers, 185-187
   web servers, 183-184
WebCrawler search engine,
   156
   see also search engines
Whiteboard (NetMeeting),
   172-173
wizards
   Channel Subscription
      Wizard, 143-145
   Internet Connection,
      configuring new servers,
      80-82
   Microsoft Publishing Wizard
      add-on, 154
   Subscription Wizard,
      131-132

Web Publishing Wizard
   FTP servers, 185-187
   web servers, 183-184
working offline, 34-35
World Wide Web
   graphics
      saving, 25-27
      using as desktop
         background, 115-116
   navigating, 7-14
      Back/Forward buttons,
         10, 20
      exploring web sites, 8-10
      favorites, 11-12
      hypertext links, 9-10
      stopping web pages, 14
      URLs, 7-8
   searching, see searches
   security, see security
   subscribing to sites, see
      subscriptions
   surfing, 13-14
   web pages, 5
      creating, see FrontPage
         Express
      customizing display,
         48-50
      favorites, see favorites
      printing, 35-37
      publishing, see publishing
         web pages
      saving, 37-38
   web sites, 5
      ActiveX controls, 160
      add-ons/plug-ins,
         155-156
      Internet Explorer 4, 155
      Museum of Modern Art,
         10
      NetShow, 162, 166-168
      search engines, 16-17,
         156, 160
      Stroud's, 160
      see also World Wide
         Web, navigating

WYSIWYG (What You See Is What You Get), 174

X-Y-Z

Yahoo! search engine, 17
  web address, 156
  see also searches, search engines

zipped (.zip) files, unzipping, 24-25

Complete and Return this Card
for a *FREE* Computer Book Catalog

Thank you for purchasing this book! You have purchased a superior computer book written expressly for your needs. To continue to provide the kind of up-to-date, pertinent coverage you've come to expect from us, we need to hear from you. Please take a minute to complete and return this self-addressed, postage-paid form. In return, we'll send you a free catalog of all our computer books on topics ranging from word processing to programming and the internet.

Mr. ☐ Mrs. ☐ Ms. ☐ Dr. ☐

Name (first) ☐☐☐☐☐☐☐☐☐ (M.I.) ☐ (last) ☐☐☐☐☐☐☐☐☐☐☐☐☐☐

Address ☐☐☐☐☐☐☐☐☐☐☐☐☐☐☐☐☐☐☐☐☐☐☐☐
☐☐☐☐☐☐☐☐☐☐☐☐☐☐☐☐☐☐☐☐☐☐☐☐

City ☐☐☐☐☐☐☐☐☐☐☐ State ☐☐ Zip ☐☐☐☐☐ ☐☐☐☐

Phone ☐☐☐ ☐☐☐ ☐☐☐☐ Fax ☐☐☐ ☐☐☐ ☐☐☐☐

Company Name ☐☐☐☐☐☐☐☐☐☐☐☐☐☐☐☐☐☐☐☐☐

E-mail address ☐☐☐☐☐☐☐☐☐☐☐☐☐☐☐☐☐☐☐☐☐☐☐☐

1. Please check at least (3) influencing factors for purchasing this book.

Front or back cover information on book .... ☐
Special approach to the content .... ☐
Completeness of content .... ☐
Author's reputation .... ☐
Publisher's reputation .... ☐
Book cover design or layout .... ☐
Index or table of contents of book .... ☐
Price of book .... ☐
Special effects, graphics, illustrations .... ☐
Other (Please specify): _____ ☐

2. How did you first learn about this book?

Internet Site .... ☐
Saw in Macmillan Computer
    Publishing catalog .... ☐
Recommended by store personnel .... ☐
Saw the book on bookshelf at store .... ☐
Recommended by a friend .... ☐
Received advertisement in the mail .... ☐
Saw an advertisement in: _____ ☐
Read book review in: _____ ☐
Other (Please specify): _____ ☐

3. How many computer books have you purchased in the last six months?

This book only .... ☐   3 to 5 books .... ☐
2 books .... ☐   More than 5 .... ☐

4. Where did you purchase this book?

Bookstore .... ☐
Computer Store .... ☐
Consumer Electronics Store .... ☐
Department Store .... ☐
Office Club .... ☐
Warehouse Club .... ☐
Mail Order .... ☐
Direct from Publisher .... ☐
Internet site .... ☐
Other (Please specify): .... ☐

5. How long have you been using a computer?

Less than 6 months .. ☐   6 months to a year ..... ☐
1 to 3 years .... ☐   More than 3 years ...... ☐

6. What is your level of experience with personal computers and with the subject of this book?

	With PC's	With subject of book
New	☐	☐
Casual	☐	☐
Accomplished	☐	☐
Expert	☐	☐

Source Code — ISBN: 0-7897-1585-6

7. Which of the following best describes your job title?

Administrative Assistant .... ☐
Coordinator .... ☐
Manager/Supervisor .... ☐
Director .... ☐
Vice President .... ☐
President/CEO/COO .... ☐
Lawyer/Doctor/Medical Professional .... ☐
Teacher/Educator/Trainer .... ☐
Engineer/Technician .... ☐
Consultant .... ☐
Not employed/Student/Retired .... ☐
Other (Please specify): .... ☐

8. Which of the following best describes the area of the company your job title falls under?

Accounting .... ☐
Engineering .... ☐
Manufacturing .... ☐
Marketing .... ☐
Operations .... ☐
Sales .... ☐
Other (Please specify): .... ☐

9. What is your age?

Under 20 .... ☐
21-29 .... ☐
30-39 .... ☐
40-49 .... ☐
50-59 .... ☐
60-over .... ☐

10. Are you:

Male .... ☐
Female .... ☐

11. Which computer publications do you read regularly? (Please list)

_____
_____
_____
_____
_____
_____
_____
_____
_____
_____
_____

Comments: _____
_____
_____
_____

Fold here and scotch-tape to m

l¹¹|¹|¹|¹|¹|¹|¹|"¹¹|¹|¹|¹|¹|¹|¹|¹|¹|¹|¹|¹|

FIRST-CLASS MAIL PERMIT NO. 9918 INDIANAPOLIS IN

POSTAGE WILL BE PAID BY THE ADDRESSEE

ATTN MARKETING
MACMILLAN COMPUTER PUBLISHING
MACMILLAN PUBLISHING USA
201 W 103RD ST
INDIANAPOLIS IN 46290-9042

NO POSTAGE
NECESSARY
IF MAILED
IN THE
UNITED STATES

Check out Que® Books on the World Wide Web
http://www.mcp.com/que

As the biggest software release in computer history, Windows 95 continues to redefine the computer industry. Click here for the latest info on our Windows 95 books

Make computing quick and easy with these products designed exclusively for new and casual users

nine the latest releases in processing, spreadsheets, ating systems, and suites

The Internet, The World Wide Web, CompuServe®, America Online®, Prodigy® —it's a world of ever-changing information. Don't get left behind!

out about new additions to site, new bestsellers and opics

In-depth information on high-end topics: find the best reference books for databases, programming, networking, and client/server technologies

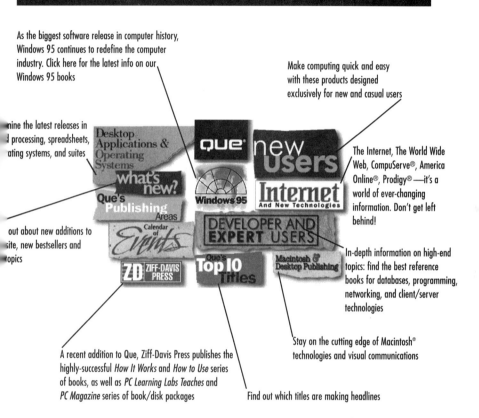

Stay on the cutting edge of Macintosh® technologies and visual communications

A recent addition to Que, Ziff-Davis Press publishes the highly-successful *How It Works* and *How to Use* series of books, as well as *PC Learning Labs Teaches* and *PC Magazine* series of book/disk packages

Find out which titles are making headlines

h 6 separate publishing groups, Que develops products for many specific market segments and areas of mputer technology. Explore our Web Site and you'll find information on best-selling titles, newly published titles, upcoming products, authors, and much more.

- Stay informed on the latest industry trends and products available
- Visit our online bookstore for the latest information and editions
- Download software from Que's library of the best shareware and freeware

Copyright © 1996, Macmillan Computer Publishing-USA, A Viacom Company

MACMILLAN COMPUTER PUBLISHING USA

A VIACOM COMPANY

Technical ---- Support:

If you need assistance with the information in this book or with a CD/Disk accompanying the book, please access the Knowledge Base on our Web site at **http://www.superlibrary.com/general/support**. Our most Frequently Asked Questions are answered there. If you do not find the answer to your questions on our Web site, you may contact Macmillan Technical Support **(317) 581-3833** or e-mail us at **support@mcp.com**.